Mastering the Fundamentals of Music

Mastering
the Fundamentals
of Music

Rebecca M. Herrold
San Jose State University

PRENTICE HALL, Upper Saddle River, New Jersey 07458

Library of Congress Cataloging-in-Publication Data

HERROLD, REBECCA.
    Mastering the fundamentals of music / by Rebecca M. Herrold.
      p. cm.
    Includes index.
    ISBN 0-13-121872-7 (pbk.)
    1. Music—Theory, Elementary.   I. Title.
MT7.H64   1997
781.2—dc20
                            96-34376
                                CIP
                                MN

Editorial director: *Charlyce Jones Owen*
Acquisitions editor: *Norwell F. Therien*
Project editor: *Carole R. Crouse*
Copy editor: *Carole R. Crouse*
Prepress and manufacturing buyer: *Bob Anderson*

This book was set in 10/12 Palatino by Thompson Type
and was printed and bound by Courier Companies, Inc.
The cover was printed by Courier Companies, Inc.

 © 1997 by Prentice-Hall, Inc.
Upper Saddle River, New Jersey 07458

Printed in the United States of America

10 9 8 7 6 5 4 3

ISBN 0-13-121872-7   (Book alone)
ISBN 0-13-263229-2   (Book with CD)
ISBN 0-13-259433-1   (CD alone)

PRENTICE-HALL INTERNATIONAL (UK) LIMITED, *London*
PRENTICE-HALL OF AUSTRALIA PTY. LIMITED, *Sydney*
PRENTICE-HALL CANADA INC., *Toronto*
PRENTICE-HALL HISPANOAMERICANA, S.A., *Mexico*
PRENTICE-HALL OF INDIA PRIVATE LIMITED, *New Delhi*
PRENTICE-HALL OF JAPAN, INC., *Tokyo*
PRENTICE-HALL ASIA PTE. LTD., *Singapore*
EDITORA PRENTICE-HALL DO BRASIL, LTDA., *Rio de Janeiro*

Contents

6   Rhythm III: Advanced Concepts   137

7   Modes and Other Scale Patterns   161

8   Intervals   177

9   Triads, Chords, and Beginning Harmony   208

Appendixes   250

Preface

Mastering the Fundamentals of Music is prepared for the pre-theory college or university class. Because no prior knowledge of music theory is prerequisite to using this text, it is also appropriate for students who need the basics of music for avocational purposes and for college preparatory classes in secondary schools.

The author believes that students best learn the basics of music through participation in musical activities: singing, listening to a variety of musics, performing rhythms, reading and notating music, composing, conducting, and completing creative and research projects on the elemental topics. To help the student accomplish these goals, each chapter includes *practice* assignments in reading, analyzing, and notating music, and *musical applications* for performing and listening. Each chapter concludes with a *list of terms* to be defined by the student and a *chapter review worksheet,* which the instructor may assign as homework or the class may complete together in preparation for an exam. The *chapter projects* may be utilized at the instructor's discretion. Some are suitable for individual work; others are appropriate for small-group collaboration.

The text is organized for maximum flexibility, so that an instructor may choose the order in which materials are presented. Chapters 1 and 2 may be presented simultaneously to introduce the basic features of both rhythm and pitch notation before more difficult rhythmic and melodic concepts are introduced. Similarly, Chapters 3 and 4, on more advanced rhythms and major keys, are compatible, since the rhythms in the examples in Chapter 4 are derived from those presented earlier. Chapter 6, Rhythm III, uses examples in minor keys, so it is dependent on the students' completion of Chapter 5, Minor Keys. The brief chapter on Modes and Additional Scales may be omitted, if time does not permit, without affecting the remaining chapters on intervals and triads.

Musical examples from European-American traditional folk and art music and world sources are presented throughout each chapter to assist students in their comprehension of basic concepts. A CD recording of sixty-plus examples related to scores in the text is available. Scores recorded on the CD are designated in the text R-1, R-2, and so on for ease of use. The selections on the CD are intended to enhance the explanations in the text. They are drawn from a broad spectrum of sources, and their presentation by the soloist or group for which they are intended—chamber ensemble, African drumming ensemble, full orchestra, and so on—adds considerably to the dimensions of musical learning addressed by the text. Examples of ethnic, nonnotated music from world sources are included for audio analysis and discussion.

To augment the offerings of the text, Appendix F lists appropriate computer-assisted music instruction programs that are available at the time of this printing. The programs include practice on note names, the circle of fifths, key signatures, major and minor scales, modes, jazz scales, scale degrees, intervals, modes, note/ rest durations, rhythm reading, rhythmic dictation, and solfege with fixed or movable *do*. The programs are useful for out-of-class practice in a laboratory setting. It must be emphasized that they do not replace classroom interaction, skill-building activities, and the text's assignments and projects as the basis for a course.

ACKNOWLEDGMENTS

I wish to thank the students in my classes at San Jose State University for their helpful comments during preparation of the manuscript. The thoughtful, practical suggestions from these professors who reviewed the text are very much appreciated: Lisa Bontrager, Penn State University; Robert L. Borg, University of Minnesota; Howard Irving, University of Alabama; Thomas Risher, University of North Alabama; Ira Paul Schwartz, State University of New York, Brockport; and Angela Yeung, University of San Diego. The diligent work of production editor Carole Crouse is highly commendable. And finally, to my husband, Stephen, my gratitude for his understanding and support during the many months devoted to this project.

Rebecca M. Herrold

Mastering
the Fundamentals
of Music

An Introduction to Rhythm

Nature provides a background of rhythms for our lives: Tides rise and fall, day turns to night, and seasons come and go. Because we humans are rhythmic creatures—our heartbeats, breathing, movements, and speech all follow natural rhythms—rhythm is the element most approachable by the student who is just beginning a formal study of music. Often, we react first to the strong, rhythmic pulses, or beats, in a piece of music. We tap our feet, snap our fingers, and sway. Therefore, in this text, we will begin our exploration of music's fundamental elements with rhythm.

Your grasp of rhythmic concepts is the foundation of future understanding of music's other elements. Successful development of musical skills is dependent on the mastery of correct rhythmic performance and requires diligent practice and application. You are asked to participate actively in the presentation of each rhythmic concept in this chapter through practice sessions, listening experiences, musical applications, and projects.

BEAT AND ACCENT

As your instructor plays a favorite march (for example, "The Stars and Stripes Forever," by John Philip Sousa, or the Bridal March from *Lohengrin*, by Richard Wagner), tap your feet and snap your fingers to its regular beats or recurring pulses.*

Tap/Snap   X   X   X   X   X   X   X   X   X   X   X   X   X   X   X   X

THE STARS AND STRIPES FOREVER (R-1)†
(excerpt)

John Philip Sousa
(United States, 1854–1932)

*Scores shown here are intended to be read by the instructor. Students begin to read notation in the section of this chapter entitled Rhythm Notation.

†R-numbers indicate titles of works that are recorded on the accompanying CD.

BRIDAL MARCH (R-2)
from *Lohengrin*
(excerpt)

Richard Wagner
(Germany, 1813–1883)

Now, as though you're marching, left-right, left-right, emphasize every other beat.

1 2 **1** 2 **1** 2 **1** 2 **1** 2 **1** 2 **1** 2 **1** 2

The strong beats, or pulses, are *accented*. The weaker beats are *unaccented*. We can show the accents and the weak beats with these symbols:

/ ᴜ / ᴜ / ᴜ / ᴜ / ᴜ / ᴜ / ᴜ / ᴜ

DUPLE METER

A regular grouping of accented and unaccented beats is called *meter*. *Duple meter* occurs when the beats are arranged in groups of two.

/ ᴜ / ᴜ / ᴜ / ᴜ / ᴜ / ᴜ / ᴜ / ᴜ
1 2 **1** 2 **1** 2 **1** 2 **1** 2 **1** 2 **1** 2 **1** 2

Chant or sing the following song lyrics in unison with your class while tapping your pen to the beats. Emphasize the strong beats. This is duple meter.

1	2
Are you slee-ping?	

1	2
Are you slee-ping?	

1	2
Bro-ther John?	

1	2
Bro-ther John?	

1	2
Mor-ning bells are ring-ing,	

1	2
Mor-ning bells are ring-ing.	

1	2
Ding, ding, dong!	

1	2
Ding, ding, dong!	

TRIPLE METER

Triple meter occurs when beats are arranged in groups of three. Listen to the following excerpts in triple meter. Tap their beats and notice the grouping of accents and weak pulses.

Accented and weak pulses in triple meter:

/ ᴜ ᴜ / ᴜ ᴜ / ᴜ ᴜ / ᴜ ᴜ / ᴜ ᴜ / ᴜ ᴜ
1 2 3 **1** 2 3 **1** 2 3 **1** 2 3 **1** 2 3 **1** 2 3

CARILLON (R-3)
from *L'Árlésienne* Suite No. 1
(excerpt, adapted score)

Georges Bizet
(France, 1838–1875)

LA DONNA È MOBILE
from *Rigoletto*

Giuseppe Verdi
(Italy, 1813−1901)

La don-na è mo - bi-le   qual piuma al ven - to   mu - ta d'ac.

ANITRA'S DANCE
from *Peer Gynt* Suite No. 1, Op. 46, III

Edvard Grieg
(Norway, 1843−1907)

Say or sing these lyrics from two songs. Again, tap the beats, emphasizing the strong ones.

1	2	3		**1**	2	3
My	coun-try			**'tis**	of	thee
1	2	3		**1**	2	3
Sweet	land	of		**li-**		ber-ty

1	2	3		**1**	2	3
La-ven-der's				**blue**	dil-ly	dil-ly
1	2	3		**1**	(2 - - - - - - -3)	
La-ven-der's				**Green**————		

QUADRUPLE METER

In *quadruple meter,* the beats are arranged in groups of four. Listen to the main themes in the following excerpts. The metrical groupings are in four, with the first and third beats having primary and secondary accents. Beats 2 and 4 are weak. Tap as you listen.

Primary and secondary accents in quadruple meter:

ODE TO JOY (R-4)
from Symphony No. 9 in D Minor

Ludwig van Beethoven
(Germany, 1770–1827)

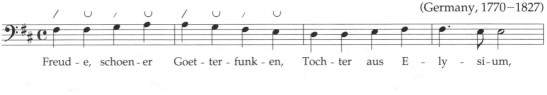

GRAND MARCH (R-5)
from *Aida*

Giuseppe Verdi
(Italy, 1813–1901)

Chant or sing these lyrics in quadruple meter. Tap the primary and secondary accents and the weak pulses as you perform.

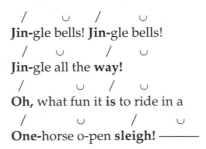

Jin-gle bells! **Jin-**gle bells!

Jin-gle all the **way!**

Oh, what fun it **is** to ride in a

One-horse o-pen **sleigh!** ———

／ ∪ ／ ∪ ／ ∪ ／ ∪
Waltz-ing Ma-til-da, waltz-ing Ma-til-da,

／ ∪ ／ ∪ ／ ∪ ／ ∪
You'll come a-waltz-ing Ma-**til-**da with me. And he

／ ∪ ／ ∪ ／ ∪ ／ ∪
Sang as he sat and **wait-**ed till his bil-ly boiled,

／ ∪ ／ ∪ ／ ∪ ／ ∪
You'll come a-waltz-ing Ma-**til-**da with me.

Now go back and perform the exercises in duple, triple, and quadruple meters (pages 2, 3, 4, and 5) by tapping your foot to the beats (primary, secondary, and weak pulses) while tapping the rhythm of the verses with your hand.

PRACTICE

Listening to and Identifying Meters

Listen as your instructor sings or plays the recordings of these works. Try to determine the patterns of accented and unaccented beats. What is the meter of each one? Is it *duple meter* (**1** 2 **1** 2 **1** 2 **1** 2), *triple meter* (**1** 2 3 **1** 2 3 **1** 2 3 **1** 2 3), or *quadruple meter* (**1** 2 3 4 **1** 2 3 4 **1** 2 3 4 **1** 2 3 4)? Write your answer in the spaces provided next to the titles.

_____ **JOY TO THE WORLD (R-6)**

George Frideric Handel
(Germany, 1685–1759)

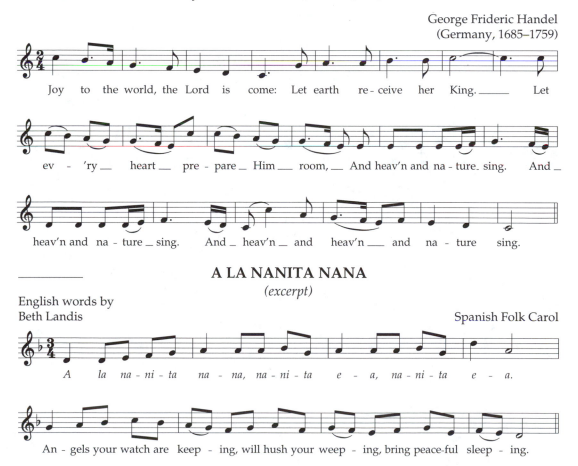

_____ **A LA NANITA NANA**
(excerpt)

English words by
Beth Landis

Spanish Folk Carol

MARCH OF THE TOREADORS
from *Carmen*
(excerpt)

Georges Bizet
(France, 1838—1875)

THIRD MOVEMENT (R-7)
from *Eine Kleine Nachtmusik*, K. 525
(excerpt)

Wolfgang Amadeus Mozart
(Austria, 1756—1791)

SECOND MOVEMENT (R-8)
from Symphony No. 94 in G Major
(theme)

Joseph Haydn
(Austria, 1732—1809)

MAZURKA IN B-FLAT MAJOR, OP. 7, NO. 1 (R-9)
(excerpt)

Frédéric Chopin
(Poland, 1810—1849)

ORANGES AND LEMONS (R-10)

(excerpt)

English Folk Song

"Oran - ges and lem - ons," say the bells of St. Clem - ents.
"Give me five far - things," say the bells of St. Mar - tins;

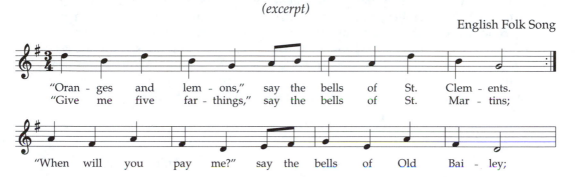

"When will you pay me?" say the bells of Old Bai - ley;

"When I grow rich," say the bells of Shore - ditch.

MUSETTE IN D (R-11)

from *Anna Magdalena Bach Notebook*
(excerpt)

Johann Sebastian Bach
(Germany, 1685−1750)

MARCH (R-12)
from *Love for Three Oranges*
(excerpt)

Sergei Prokofiev
(Russia, 1891–1953)

Now that you are familiar with *beat, accent,* and *meter* in music, you are prepared to begin reading music notation. Since music occurs across time, you will first be introduced to the appearance of music symbols of time called *notes* and the ways notes are organized in meters and *measures.*

RHYTHM NOTATION

Music has its own written language that allows sounds and their durations to be notated. Although much of the world's music is passed from person to person and place to place without notation, Western music is often written to preserve it through the centuries and to allow wide dissemination. (Exceptions to this are jazz and rock, which often call for performers to improvise.) Notation allows composers to indicate how they intend their music to sound and gives performers access to huge repertories of music that could not possibly be kept in human memory.

The Note

The musician has two musical systems to read: rhythm notation and pitch notation. (In this chapter, we will focus on rhythm notation.) The principal symbol used to convey a sound and its duration is the *note.* The parts of a note are shown below. Study the parts that are relevant to duration.

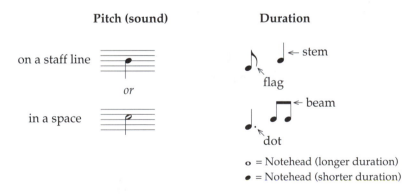

Duration and Relative Note Values

Duration in music refers to the length of time that a sound is sustained by a voice or an instrument. Notes have durations that are *relative* to one another, with the whole note, a white ellipse, assigned a value of 1. Equal to the whole note are two half notes, four quarter notes, eight eighth notes, sixteen sixteenth notes, and thirty-two thirty-second notes. The speed at which music is performed does not alter these relationships.

Note Names   Notation

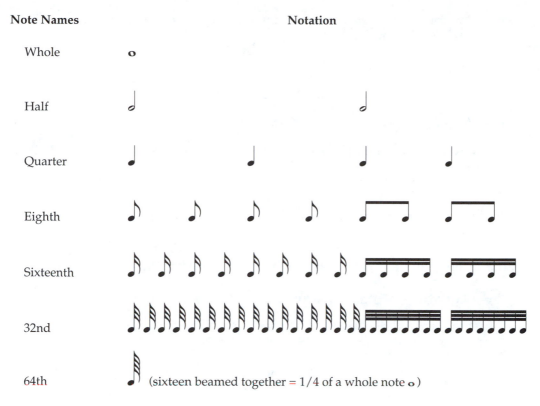

Whole   o

Half

Quarter

Eighth

Sixteenth

32nd

64th   (sixteen beamed together = 1/4 of a whole note o)

Study the preceding list and relate it to these statements:

1. If the quarter note receives one beat, the half note is worth two beats and the whole note receives four beats.
2. If the eighth note is worth one beat, the quarter note is worth two beats and the sixteenth note receives one-half beat.
3. If the half note is worth one beat, the whole note is equal to two beats and the quarter note receives one-half beat.

Measure, Bar Line, and Double Bar Line

Practice tapping out the following notes. In this example, let the quarter note equal one beat. There are sixteen beats altogether.

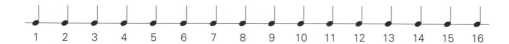

1 2 3 4 5 6 7 8 9 10 11 12 13 14 15 16

Notice that it is difficult to keep your place with so many notes in succession. To make reading easier, notes are grouped according to meter into *measures*. Here is the same exercise divided into four measures of four beats. Note that two vertical lines are used to conclude the exercise. Numbers for counting the rhythm aloud are shown.

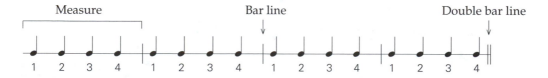

Measure   Bar line   Double bar line

1 2 3 4   1 2 3 4   1 2 3 4   1 2 3 4

Now tap out an exercise in which the half note equals one beat and there are two beats in a measure.

Repeat Sign

In this exercise, the eighth note receives one beat and there are three beats in a measure.

The ‖: and :‖ indicate that the last two measures are to be repeated.

Time Signature (Meter Signature)

The performer reads the *time signature* (or *meter signature*) at the beginning of each piece of music in order to know

    4   the number of beats per measure (meter)
    4   the kind of note that equals one beat (♩)

Sometimes, the bottom number in a time signature is replaced with the note that is equal to one beat.

    4   beats per measure
    ♩   the quarter note equals one beat

Study the following meter signatures and their interpretations.

    2   beats per measure
    2   the half note equals one beat

    2   beats per measure
    ♩   the half note equals one beat

    3   beats per measure
    8   the eighth note equals one beat

    3   beats per measure
    ♪   the eighth note equals one beat

SIMPLE METERS

In simple meters, the beat is divided into two equal parts.

Counting in Simple Meters:
Beats, Divided Beats, and Subdivided Beats

Musicians use combinations of numbers and syllables to count aloud the rhythms they will sing or play. Count aloud the following rhythms using the numbers and syllables indicated.

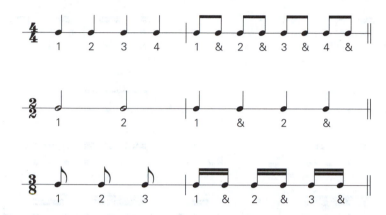

Further subdivisions use the numbers and syllables this way:

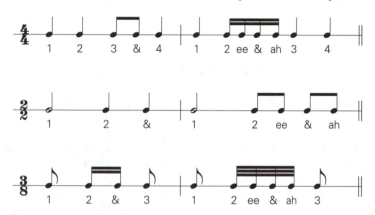

When we count the beat numbers and use syllables to indicate their divisions and subdivisions, we are using a system for speaking the rhythm of a piece of music.

PRACTICE

Reading and Playing in Simple Meters

Tapping the beats with your foot, count out each line of rhythm saying the beats, divided beats, and subdivided beats. Then tap them, or play them on percussion instruments, on one key of a keyboard, or on one recorder pitch.

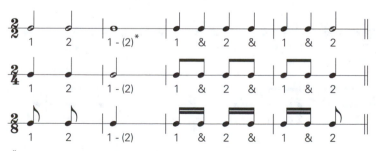

*1 - (2): Say the first number and sustain it through the second number.

PRACTICE

Aural Identification of Rhythms in Simple Meters

Number these examples in the order they are performed for you.

PRACTICE

Writing Meter Signatures and Counting in Simple Meters

Study each example; then write an appropriate meter signature in the blank space. Also write the counting numbers and the division/subdivision syllables under the notes.

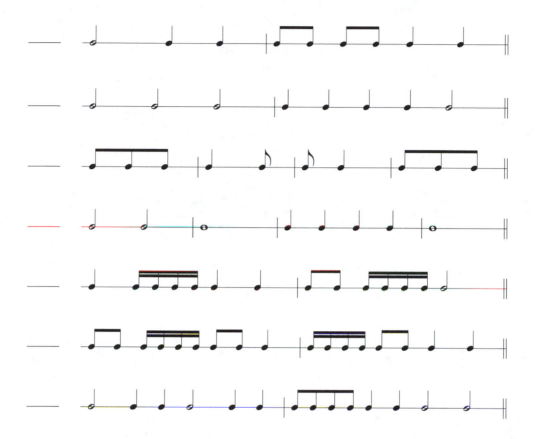

MUSICAL APPLICATION

Singing with Whole, Half, Quarter, and Eighth Notes

Tap the rhythm of each song. Then sing it with your class.

GOOD KING WENCESLAS (R-13)

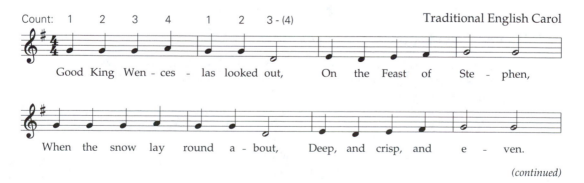

(continued)

Bright - ly shone the moon that night, Though the frost was cru – el,

When a poor man came in sight, Gath-'ring win - ter fu – – el.

YANKEE DOODLE
(excerpt)

U.S.A.

Count: 1 & 2 & 1 & 2 & 1 & 2 & 1 2

Yan - kee Doo - dle went to town a - ri - ding on a po - ny,

Stuck a fea - ther in his cap and called it mac - a - ro - ni.

Sing on "loo."

LONG, LONG AGO

Count: 1 2 & 3 4 & 1 2 & 3 - (4)

Fine

*D.C. al Fine**

> **D.C. al Fine* (*Da Capo al Fine*) directs the performer to return to the beginning and continue to *Fine* (end).

Common Time and Cut Time *(Alla Breve)*

Two time signatures that have survived from an early system of notation are *common time*, designated by the symbol ℭ; and *alla breve*, designated by the symbol ¢ (also called *cut time*).

The symbol ℭ indicates that the score should be read in $\frac{4}{4}$, whereas the symbol ¢ indicates a meter of $\frac{2}{2}$.

Tap each example as you count using numbers.

1   2   3   4   1 - (2)   3 - (4)   1   2   3   4   1 - (4)

MUSICAL APPLICATION

Singing in Simple Meters

Study these songs in simple meters, focusing on the note values, time signatures, and measures. Count aloud the rhythm of each one, and then sing the songs with your instructor's assistance. Listen to the relative durations in the rhythm.

JIM-ALONG, JOSIE

American Folk Song

1. Hi, come a-long, Jim-a-long, Jo-sie! Hi!, come a-long, Jim-a-long, Joe!

Hi, come a-long, Jim-a-long, Jo-sie! Hi, come-a-long, Jim-a-long, Joe!

SAKURA

Japanese Folk Song

Sa-ku-ra, Sa-ku-ra, Ya-yo-i-no so-ra-wa. Mi-wa-ta-su

ka-gi-ri. Ka-su-mi-ka I-za-ya, i-za-ya, Mi - ni___ yu-ka-n.

Translation:

Sakura, Sakura,
‖: Pretty blossoms ev'rywhere.
Perfume fills the soft spring air. :‖
Cherry blossoms pink and white,
Pink and white.
We can see them on our way.

AH, POOR BIRD

Traditional Round

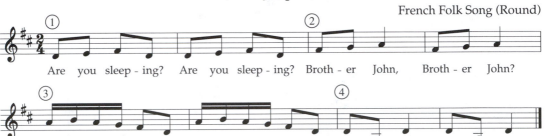

Ah,   poor bird,   Take   your flight,   Far   a-bove the sor - rows of   this   dark night.

ARE YOU SLEEPING?
(Frère Jacques)

French Folk Song (Round)

Are   you   sleep - ing?   Are   you   sleep - ing? Broth - er   John,   Broth - er   John?

Morn-ing bells are ring - ing,   morn-ing bells are ring-ing,   Ding, ding, dong!   Ding, ding, dong!

Pronunciation Guide:

Frère Jacques! Frère Jacques!
freh-reh jhah-keh freh-reh jhah-keh
Dormez vous? Dormez vous?
dor-may voo dor-may voo
Sonnez les matines, Sonnez les matines,
soh-nay lay mah-tee-neh soh-nay lay mah-tee-neh
Din, din don! Din, din, don!
dihn dihn dawn dihn dihn dawn

ON THE BRIDGE AT AVIGNON

France

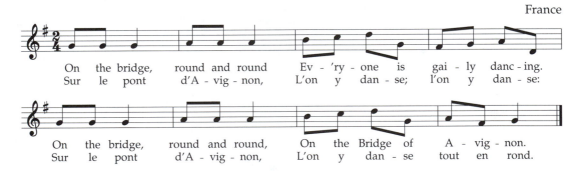

On   the bridge,   round and round   Ev - 'ry - one   is   gai - ly   danc - ing.
Sur   le   pont   d'A - vig - non,   L'on   y   dan - se;   l'on   y   dan - se:

On   the bridge,   round and round,   On   the   Bridge   of   A - vig - non.
Sur   le   pont   d'A - vig - non,   L'on   y   dan - se   tout   en   rond.

PRACTICE

Writing Notation

Practice writing notes as they appear here. Observe that the notehead is an oval slanted to the right. Most notes have stems, which extend up from the right side of the notehead or down from the left side of the notehead.

Flags curve to the right whether the stems go up or down.

Beams are used to group notes of the same duration.

PRACTICE

Correcting Incomplete and Incorrectly Notated Measures

Study these examples. Then complete each incomplete measure with appropriate notes.

Rewrite each line. Place beams where appropriate over the divisions and subdivisions. Add measure lines.

Eighth/Sixteenth-Note Subdivisions

Tap out each line with your instructor while counting aloud. In the last line of each example, you will be introduced to a new beat subdivision.

Eighth/ Sixteenth-Note Combination   **Sixteenth/ Eighth-Note Combination**

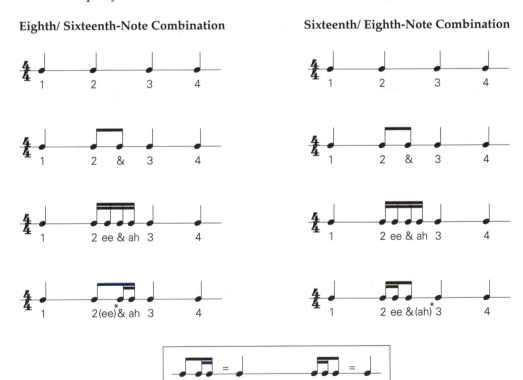

* The (ee) and the (ah) are not spoken.

PRACTICE

Counting Eighth/Sixteenth-Note Combinations

Count each line aloud with your class.

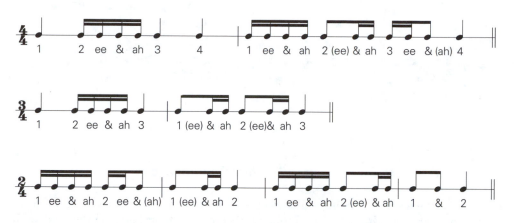

MUSICAL APPLICATION

Singing Songs with Eighth/Sixteenth-Note Combinations

Listen as your instructor presents the following songs. Tap or clap the rhythm in each song as it is played or sung. Then practice counting the rhythm patterns in the first four measures of each example. Finally, sing the songs, giving special attention to the new patterns.

SKIP TO MY LOU
(excerpt)

American Folk Song

1. Fly's in the but-ter-milk, shoo, fly, shoo!   Fly's in the but-termilk, shoo, fly, shoo!

Fly's in the but-ter-milk, shoo, fly, shoo!   Skip to my Lou, my   dar - ling.

CAROL OF THE BIRDS

Catalonia

See how the No - el   star shines bright!   But what is that   I   hear   to - night?

A   flock of lit - tle   birds it's   true,   fly - ing to Beth - l'hem   two   by   two.

WHAT'LL I DO WITH THE BABY-O?

American Fiddle Tune

What-'ll I do with the ba - by - O?   What-'ll I   do with the   ba - by - O?

What-'ll I   do with the   ba - by - O?   If he don't go   to   sleep - y - O?

MUSICAL APPLICATION

Listening to Eighth/Sixteenth-Note Combinations

These excerpts from instrumental works include eighth/sixteenth-note combinations. Tap the rhythm of each one while counting and keeping the beat with your foot. Then listen to the examples. Count and tap again.

LES BALLET DES REVENANTS, OP. 5 (R-14)

Clara Schumann
(Germany, 1819—1896)

MOMENT MUSICAL, OP. 94, NO. 3

Franz Schubert
(Austria, 1797–1828)

*Grace note. Played quickly—not counted in the rhythm of the piece.

PRACTICE

Creating, Counting, and Performing Rhythms with Eighth/Sixteenth-Note Combinations

Rewrite each line. Divide two of the eighth-note groups in each line into some combination of eighth/sixteenth-note patterns. Then write out the counting numbers and syllables for each new line. Finally, tap them out or sing them on one syllable.

MUSICAL APPLICATION

Listening to Music in Simple Meters

The following musical works are written in simple meters and are made up of basic note values and their divisions. As you listen to them, follow the notational examples. Then, when you have finished listening to the excerpts, clap the rhythms in the examples.

PRELUDE TO ACT 1
from *Hansel and Gretel* (Opera)

Engelbert Humperdinck
(Germany, 1854–1921)

VALSE, OP. 34, NO. 2 (R-15)

Frédéric Chopin
(Poland, 1810–1849)

VARIATIONS AND FUGUE ON A THEME OF PURCELL (R-16)
from *The Young Person's Guide to the Orchestra*

Benjamin Britten
(England, 1913–1976)

Listen to **Pobin Poa Si Li Tan (R-17),** music from Indonesia. Can you find the beats in the music? Are they grouped in twos, threes, or fours? Are there divisions and subdivisions of the basic beat?

REVIEW OF TERMS

Define each term. Where appropriate, draw, notate, or use in a musical context to demonstrate your understanding.

1. beat
2. accent
3. duple meter
4. triple meter
5. quadruple meter
6. duration
7. notehead
8. stem
9. flag
10. beam
11. dot
12. relative note values
13. measure
14. bar line
15. double bar line
16. repeat sign
17. *D.C. al Fine*
18. time signature
19. meter signature
20. divided beat
21. subdivided beat
22. *alla breve*
23. cut time
24. common time
25. whole note
26. half note
27. quarter note
28. eighth note
29. sixteenth note
30. thirty-second note

WORSHEET
Chapter 1 Review

1. Mark strong and weak accents over the X's to show duple, triple, and quadruple meters. Write beat numbers under the X's.

X X X X X X X X   Duple meter

X X X X X X X X X   Triple Meter

X X X X X X X X   Quadruple Meter

2. Define *meter.* _____

3. Name the two musical systems that musicians read: _____

and _____

4. What does a *note* indicate to the musician? _____

5. Name each part of the notes indicated by arrows.

_____   _____   _____   _____

6. Correct the notes that are incorrectly drawn.

_____

7. In *relative duration,* the whole note is assigned a value of _____.

8. On a separate sheet, make a chart showing the relative durations of *whole, half, quarter, eighth, sixteenth,* and *thirty-second notes.*

9. How many measures are there in a performance of this example?

Fine

D.C. al Fine

10. Draw measure lines and double bar lines where they are needed.

CHAPTER PROJECTS

1. Tap this rhythm, observing the accents carefully. Can you create a verse (lyrics) from it? (You may change any ⊓ to ⊓⊓ or ⊓⊓.)

2. Working in a small group, perform these two-part simple-meter rhythms in an ensemble. Use percussion instruments or, with two performers, these notes on a keyboard:

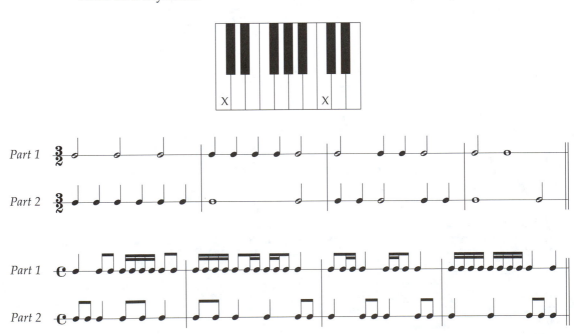

An Introduction to Pitch and the Keyboard

PITCH AND MELODY

A *pitch* is sound created when vocal cords, a string, or metal vibrates at a specific frequency. Slower vibrations produce lower pitches; faster vibrations generate higher pitches. To gain an understanding of the concept of higher and lower pitches, go to a piano and pluck one of the longest strings (on the left side of the instrument), then one of the shortest strings (on the right side of the instrument). You can observe that the long string vibrates more slowly and emits a lower pitch; the short string vibrates faster and produces a higher pitch.

Another experiment you can conduct to produce higher and lower pitches, or tones, involves filling glasses of the same size with varying amounts of water. When you tap the rims, which glasses produce lower tones? Higher tones? If you experiment with a mallet instrument (a xylophone, for example), which bars produce the higher tones and which the lower tones? By now, you are finding that the smaller the string, glass, or piece of metal in vibration, the higher the pitch will be.

The musical element we call *melody* is made up of a planned series of pitches with varying durations. You'll remember from Chapter 1 that these durations are collectively referred to as rhythm, and you learned about rhythm notation. Next we will discuss pitch notation.

PITCH NOTATION

Although most of the world's music is not written and relies on rote learning and memory for its continued existence, much of Western music is notated by composers and re-created by performers who read it.

The Staff

The idea of notating pitches on a *staff* of lines and spaces is almost one thousand years old. An Italian monk, Guido d'Arezzo (d. 1050), devised a system of pitch notation using lines that allowed church music to be written, transported from one place to another, and passed on from one generation to the next. Over the centuries, many elaborations have enhanced those first efforts, including the development of mensural notation, with its stems, beams, dots, flags, and rests that permit us to read both pitch and rhythm.

The notational system that we have inherited from many generations of composers and theorists employs five lines upon which we place pitches. The five lines are called the *staff. The lines and spaces are numbered from the bottom up.*

The Musical Alphabet and the Clef

Each pitch is assigned a letter name, and only the first seven letters of the alphabet are used in the *musical alphabet* (A–G). A *clef* appears at the beginning of the staff to assign a specific letter name to each line and space. There are three clefs, representing the pitches G, F, and C. These are known as the G clef, the F clef, and the C clef.

The G Clef

The *G clef,* also known as the *treble clef,* is used to notate scores for children's voices and for soprano, alto, and tenor adult voices. In instrumental music, this clef is used in scores for higher-pitched instruments (for example, violin, flute, clarinet, oboe, trumpet, French horn, glockenspiel) and for the right half of keyboard instruments.

The circle at the bottom of the treble clef encloses the G line and thereby shows the location of G on the staff. The other pitches are lettered accordingly, and the next letter after G is A, since the seven-letter alphabet is repeated. The letter before G in the alphabet is F. Note the placement of F, G, and A.

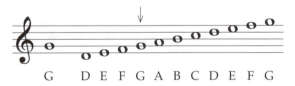

Positions of Notes on Lines and Spaces

Adjacent letters of the alphabet are placed on adjacent lines and spaces. For example, the progression A–B–C moves from the second space up to the third line, then up to the third space. The progression C–B–A moves down from the third space to the third line, then down to the second space. Study the following example. Ascending pitches are identified by the letters moving forward alphabetically; descending pitches employ the letters moving backward.

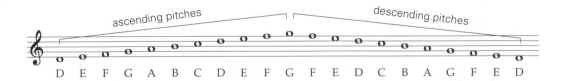

Listen as your instructor plays the preceding example. Hum along with the piano or voice, and point to the notes as they sound.

Ledger Lines

Pitches sounding beyond the scope of the five-line staff are written upon *ledger lines* either below the first line or above the fifth line.

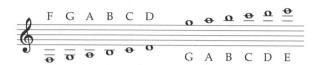

PRACTICE

Writing Letter Names of Notes with the G Clef

Write the letter names of the notes on the lines below the staff.

Listen as your instructor plays the preceding pitches on a keyboard for you. Point to the notes, and relate what you are hearing to their higher or lower positions on the staff.

PRACTICE

Notating Octaves with the G Clef

A pitch that vibrates twice as fast as another is at the distance of an *octave* above it and has the same letter name. Draw an octave that corresponds to each letter shown below. The first one is done for you.

E   B G A D F C

The F Clef

The clef used for lower-pitched voices and instruments (for example, cello, string bass, tuba) and for the left half of keyboard instruments is the *F clef,* also referred to as the *bass clef.* Observe that G is in the space above F, since G follows F alphabetically. The note E is in the space below F because E precedes F alphabetically.

F   F G A B C D E F G A B

As with the treble clef, ledger lines are used to expand the staff.

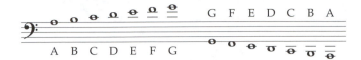

Ottava (*8va*)

A series of notes written on more than two ledger lines is difficult to read. The symbol *8va*, which stands for *ottava* (Italian, meaning "eight"), is used to aid the performer. It indicates that the notes are to be played one octave higher or lower than written, thereby eliminating the need for ledger lines. Study the following examples.

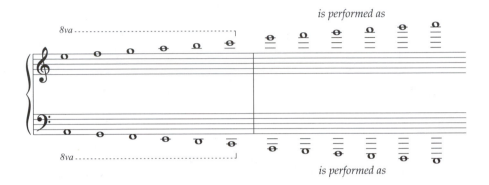

PRACTICE

Writing Letter Names of Notes with the F Clef

Write the letter names of these pitches.

Listen as your instructor plays the preceding pitches on a keyboard for you. Point to the notes, and relate what you are hearing to their higher or lower positions on the staff.

PRACTICE

Notating Octaves with the F Clef

Draw an octave that corresponds to each letter shown here. The first one is done for you.

B   G A D F C E

The C Clefs

The five C clefs are soprano, mezzo soprano, alto, tenor, and baritone. Although C clefs were in common use for both vocal and instrumental music of earlier periods, only two survive in contemporary scores—the alto and the tenor clefs. The alto C clef is used for the viola; the tenor C clef is used for the trombone, the bassoon, and the cello. As the name indicates, the C clef designates the location of middle C on the staff. (Middle C on the piano is approximately in the center of the keyboard.)

Alto C Clef
Middle C

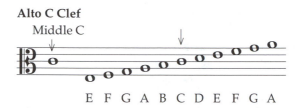

E F G A B C D E F G A

Tenor C Clef
Middle C

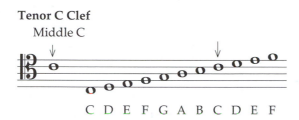

C D E F G A B C D E F

Your ability to read C clefs will be important if you wish to perform early music or work with orchestral scores.

PRACTICE

Writing Letter Names of Notes with C Clefs

Write the letter names of the notes shown after each C clef.

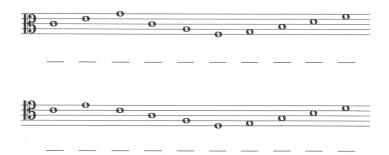

___ ___ ___ ___ ___ ___ ___ ___ ___ ___

___ ___ ___ ___ ___ ___ ___ ___ ___ ___

Draw the clefs following the directions given below.

Treble clef: Draw a vertical line.

Draw an oval at the top of the line, ending at the fourth staff line.

Complete the clef by extending the curved line in a circle that rests on the bottom line.

Bass clef: Draw a dot on the fourth line.	Draw a curved line upward to the top line and a half circle to the right, extending down to the second line.	Add two dots, one above and one below the fourth line.

C clef: Draw two vertical lines, one heavy, one light.	Draw a half circle, ending at the line you wish to designate as C.

PRACTICE

Listening for Higher and Lower Pitches

As your instructor plays these pairs of pitches for you, indicate which pitch is higher (H) and which is lower (L). If the pitch repeats, mark the second one with an R.

1.

_____   _____

2.

_____   _____

3.
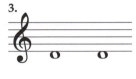

_____   _____

4.
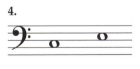

_____   _____

5.
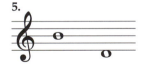

_____   _____

6.
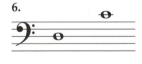

_____   _____

7.
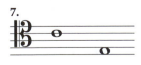

_____   _____

8.
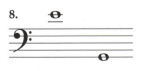

_____   _____

PRACTICE

Writing Notes in G, F, and C Clefs

Write the notes associated with the letter names. When a letter is repeated, show two note placements on the staff.

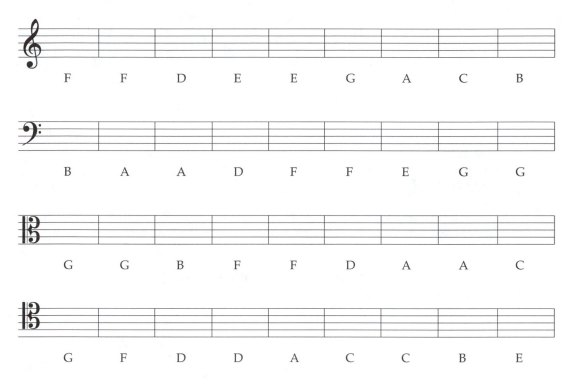

Identify the letter name of each note. Then write a note with the same letter name in the different clef.

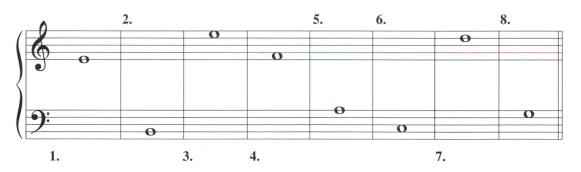

Write the bass-clef notes that represent the same pitches as the alto-clef notes.

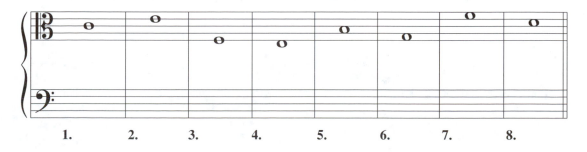

Write the tenor-clef notes that represent the same pitches as the bass-clef notes.

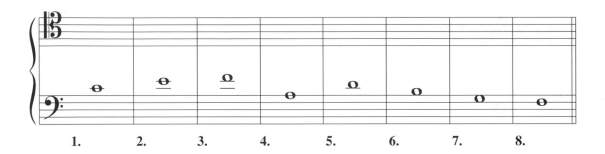

1.   2.   3.   4.   5.   6.   7.   8.

PRACTICE

Identifying Letter Names of Notes in Songs

Write the letter names above the notes in these songs. The first measure of each is done for you. Then hum each example with your instructor's assistance.

UNTO US A BOY IS BORN

Fifteenth-Century Carol

C   D   E   F   __   __   __   __   __   __   __   __   __   __   __   __

THIS OLD MAN

Traditional

G   E   G   __   __   __   __   __   __   __   __   __   __

This old man,   he played one,   He played knick-knack   on   my   drum.

Knick-knack pad-dy-whack, give a dog a bone,   This old man came roll - ing home.

MUSICAL APPLICATION

Combining Rhythm and Pitch to Make Melodies

Part A
1. Tap out this rhythm.

2. Now study this sequence of pitches.

3. If we assign the pitches in step 2 to the durations in step 1, we will re-create a melody that is recognizable. The rhythm is not a song without the pitches, and the series of pitches means little without the rhythm.

Part B
1. Here is the rhythm of a well-known nursery tune.

2. If we assign a pitch to each duration, we create the melody associated with the rhythm.

PRACTICE

Assigning Rhythm to a Sequence of Pitches

This sequence of pitches is derived from a graduation march.

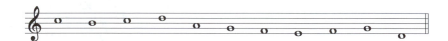

With your instructor's guidance, transform the pitches above into a melody by assigning them their correct rhythmic durations.

POMP AND CIRCUMSTANCE

Sir Edward Elgar
(England, 1857–1934)

THE KEYBOARD

A practical audiovisual aid in the study of melodic and harmonic concepts is the keyboard. You may use a traditional piano or a smaller electronic keyboard. The keyboard at the back of this text can serve as a handy visual reference.

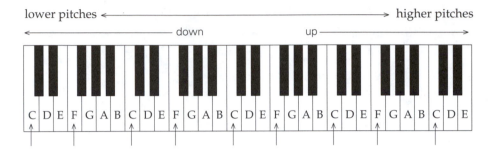

The White Keys

Note that the musical alphabet A–G is repeated in naming the white keys. The letter C is always assigned to the key immediately to the left of the two black keys. The letter F is always assigned to the key immediately to the left of the three black keys.

PRACTICE

Writing Letter Names of Keyboard Keys

Write the letter names of the keys marked X.

1.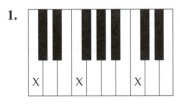

2.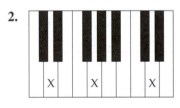

3.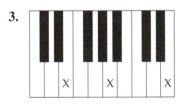

4.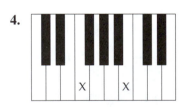

The Grand Staff

The *grand staff* is a double staff that includes a treble clef and a bass clef. All the frequently used pitches can be written on this staff. Middle C is placed between the two staves. The grand staff can be considered an eleven-line staff with middle C occupying the short eleventh line.

PIANO KEYBOARD

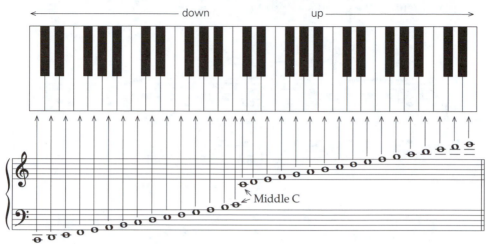

Grand Staff

The grand staff is used primarily for piano scores. It is also found in vocal and instrumental solos with keyboard accompaniments and in four-part choral music. In piano music, the right hand is assigned to the treble clef and the left hand to the bass clef.

Right hand

Left hand

VOCAL SOLO WITH KEYBOARD ACCOMPANIMENT

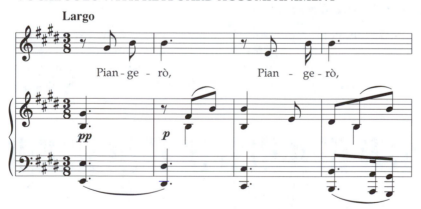

FOUR-PART CHORAL SCORE

Middle C and other notes common to both clefs are performed according to their placement on the grand staff.

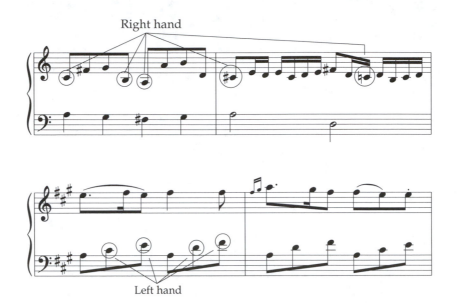

NOTES COMMON TO BOTH CLEFS

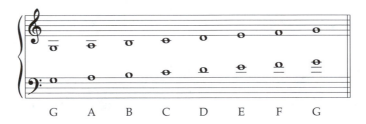

G   A   B   C   D   E   F   G

Keyboard Octave Designations

The musical alphabet is repeated several times on the standard piano keyboard. To help locate a specific pitch for a letter name, numbers are assigned to the pitches in each octave. In one system, the pitch middle C is found in the middle of the keyboard and is numbered c^4. Observe how the other number groupings are arranged at the keyboard.

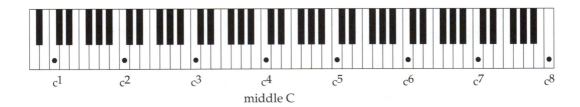

The notes between c^1 and c^2 are all named with the number 1, including d^1, e^1, f^1, g^1, a^1, b^1. Between c^2 and c^3, all the notes are named with the number 2, including d^2, e^2, f^2, and so on.

In notation, the octave designations appear this way:

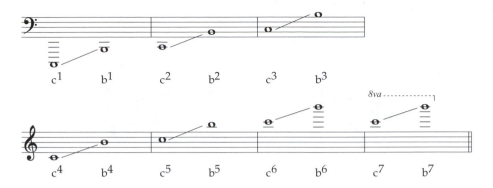

c¹   b¹   c²   b²   c³   b³

c⁴   b⁴   c⁵   b⁵   c⁶   b⁶   c⁷   b⁷

The three notes below c^1 are designated b, $b^\flat$, and a with no numbers. The c following c^7 is designated c^8.

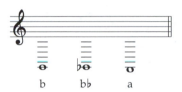

b   b♭   a

PRACTICE

Write the letter name of each note followed by its octave designation number. Play each one on a piano.

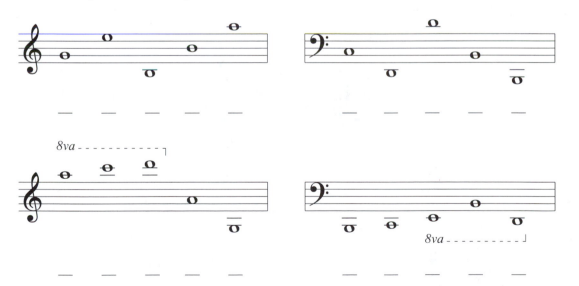

Half Steps and Whole Steps

The half step is the smallest distance between two notes in Western music. Distances smaller than half steps are perceived to be "out of tune," although much of the world's music comprises intervals smaller than half steps.

Half steps can be identified easily on a keyboard: The distance between any two adjacent keys is a half step. A distance comprising two half steps is a whole step.

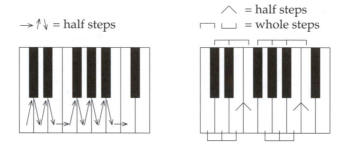

The Black Keys

Each black key on the keyboard has two related white keys. D can be raised a half step to D♯ (D-sharp). E can be lowered a half step to E♭ (E-flat). The D♯ and the E♭ sound identical on the keyboard but have different functions in musical notation, which we shall cover in the section on scales. These notes are called *enharmonic* pitches.

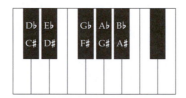

Where there is no black key between white keys, the adjacent white keys must be used to raise (sharp) or lower (flat) a pitch. E♯ is the same as the white note F, and F♭ is the same as the white note E. Similarly, B♯ is the same as the white note C, and C♭ is the same as the white note B.

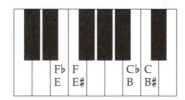

PRACTICE

Identifying Half Steps and Whole Steps

Identify each interval as a half step (H) or a whole step (W).

1. A–B _____

2. C♯–D♯ _____

3. F–E _____

4. D♯–E♯ _____

5. C–B _____

6. A♭–G♭ _____

7. E–D _____

8. B♭–C _____

9. F♯–G _____

10. E♯–F♯ _____

PRACTICE

Writing Enharmonic Names and Notes

Write the name of the enharmonic pitch for each pitch listed below.

C♯ _____	D♯ _____
A♭ _____	F♭ _____
C♭ _____	D♭ _____
E♯ _____	G♭ _____
F♯ _____	B _____
G♯ _____	E♭ _____

NOTATING AND SPEAKING THE NAMES OF ACCIDENTALS

An *accidental* is a sign used to alter a pitch for one measure.

Sharps and Flats

The *sharp* raises a pitch one half step. The *flat* lowers a pitch one half step. When we write a flat (♭) or a sharp (♯) on the staff, it always appears *before* the note it alters. The accidental is placed directly on the line or in the space of the note following it. Observe the placement of the ♭ and the ♯ in these examples:

When we say the name of a sharped or a flatted note, we say the name of the accidental *after* the letter name of the note, as in "B-flat" or "D-sharp" (not "flat B" or "sharp D").

Other Note Alterations

You have learned that the sharp raises a pitch by a half step and the flat lowers a pitch by a half step. There are other alterations, used less frequently but, nonetheless, necessary for the correct spelling of some scales.

The *double sharp* (𝄪) raises a pitch by a whole step.
The *double flat* (♭♭) lowers a pitch by a whole step.
The *natural* (♮) cancels all other accidentals.

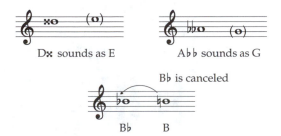

D𝄪 sounds as E   A♭♭ sounds as G

B♭ is canceled

B♭   B

PRACTICE

Working with Accidentals

1. Notate each pitch with its accidental. (Do not use ledger lines for note placement.) Then, beside the notation, write the spoken version of what you have notated.

Pitch	Notation	Spoken Version
A♯		_____
D♭		_____
F𝄪		_____
G♭♭		_____
E♯		_____

2. Above each note, write its letter name, including accidentals, if any, and its   designation. The first one is done for you.

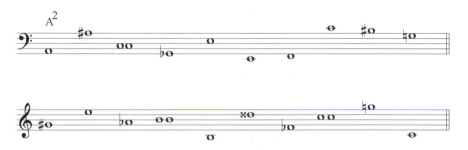

3. On the keyboard, write the name of each note listed below. Designate black keys by writing the note name(s) above the keys.

F♯   E♭

C♭   D

G𝄪   C♯

A♮   D♯

B   G♭

4. Beside each note, write its enharmonic equivalent.

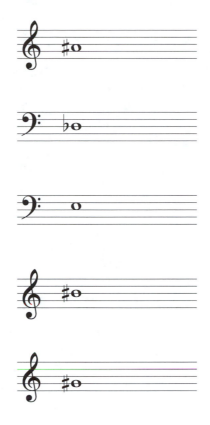

MELODIC CONTOUR

A melody has a contour that can be drawn as an iconic representation of its pitches. The horizontal direction of notes on a staff shows pitches staying in the same place, moving up, or moving down. Those that move up or down do so by step, skip, or leap. Study these songs and the contour of each as depicted below it.

ROCKY MOUNTAIN

U.S.A.

CHARLIE OVER THE OCEAN

THE STAR-SPANGLED BANNER
(excerpt)

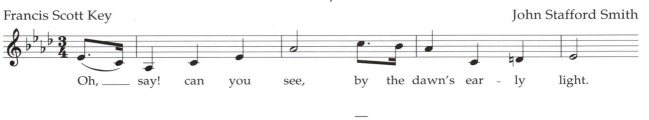

REVIEW OF TERMS

Define each term. Where appropriate, draw, notate, or use in a musical context to demonstrate your understanding.

1. pitch
2. melody
3. staff
4. musical alphabet
5. G clef
6. treble clef
7. F clef
8. bass clef
9. C clef
10. alto clef
11. tenor clef
12. ledger line
13. octave
14. keyboard
15. white keys
16. grand staff
17. octave designations
18. *8va*
19. half step
20. whole step
21. black keys
22. sharp
23. flat
24. enharmonic pitches
25. double sharp
26. double flat
27. natural
28. melodic contour

WORKSHEET
Chapter 2 Review

Answer each question.

1. What is a pitch and how is it created?

_____

_____

2. What creates a high pitch? A low pitch?

_____

_____

3. Name any pitch. _____

4. Name any melody. _____

5. Name the four clefs in common use today: _____, _____, _____, and _____.

6. What are ledger lines?_____

_____

7. Draw an example of a ledger line on the staff. Draw a note on or around the ledger line, and write its alphabetical name above or below it.

8. How are ascending pitches related to the musical alphabet A–G?

_____

9. How are descending pitches related to the musical alphabet A–G?

_____

10. Draw the clef that is used to notate music for lower-pitched voices and instruments, including the string bass and the tuba.

11. Draw the clef that is used to notate music for higher-pitched voices and instruments, including the flute and the violin.

12. Draw the clef that is used to notate music for the viola.

13. Draw the clef that is sometimes used to notate music for the trombone, the bassoon, and the cello.

14. Write the letter name of each note on the staves below.

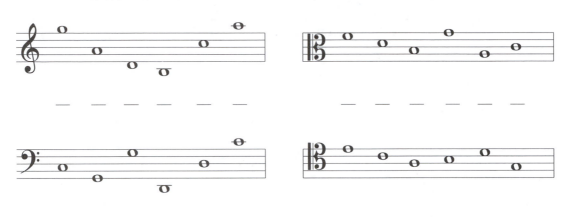

15. Write the letter name and the numerical octave designation under each key marked X. The location of middle C is shown.

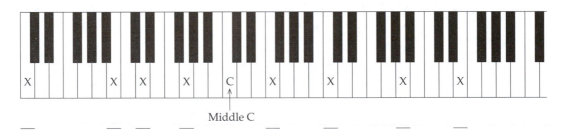

Middle C

16. What is the smallest distance between two pitches, or notes, in Western music?

_____

17. Which pairs of pitches are *enharmonic?*

E F♭   D♯ E♭   A♭ G♯   C♭ B   F♯ E♯

18. Write the names of the enharmonic notes associated with each of the black keys.

19. Each arrow connects two notes, creating a step. Write an H in the space when a half step is shown; write a W when a whole step is shown.

— — — — — — —

20. Create a grand staff from the staves below. Draw a clef at the beginning of each staff; then draw middle C from the arrows between the two staves. Complete the grand staff by drawing ascending notes on each line and in each space. In the area beneath each staff, write the letter names of the notes.

Middle C

CHAPTER PROJECTS

1. Write these pitches as whole notes on the grand staff. Note the octave designations.

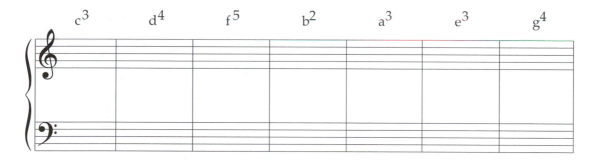

2. Locate the notes for these songs on the white keys of a keyboard.

"Ah, Poor Bird," p. 16

"Sakura," p. 15

"What'll I Do with the Baby-O?" p. 20

3. Draw the melodic contour of one of these selections.

"Unto Us a Boy Is Born," p. 32

"On the Bridge at Avignon," p. 16

"Carol of the Birds," p. 19

Rhythm II: The Basics Continued

Chapter 3 will expand your ability to read rhythm notation. You will learn the symbols for silence, called rests, and work with uneven patterns of sounds notated with dotted notes. Many practice exercises, songs, and listening selections chosen from a global perspective will enhance your ability to work with rhythm in a variety of musical settings.

RESTS

Melody includes a series of sounds and silences. The duration of silence is expressed in symbols called *rests*. The symbol is equivalent in durational value to a note, and it tells the performer to be silent for the duration of that note. The following chart shows you the relative values of rests and their equivalent notes.

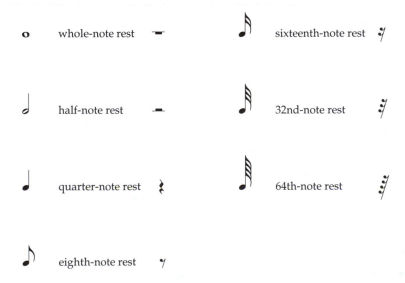

This example shows the correct placement of rests on a staff.

Correct and Incorrect Placement of Rests

Whole notes are used to indicate a full measure of silence, even if the meter is $\frac{2}{4}$, $\frac{3}{4}$, or a compound meter we shall study later in the text. Quarter rests, rather than half rests, are used in $\frac{3}{4}$ meter to assist the performer in achieving accuracy in counting. Half rests are not used in the middle of a measure in $\frac{4}{4}$.

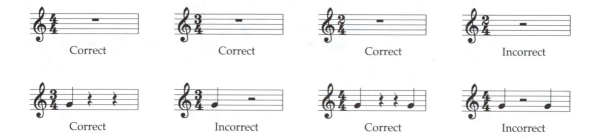

PRACTICE

Writing and Counting Rests

Use one of the rests shown on page 46 to complete each measure.

Write one note and one rest that equals the duration of the notes shown.

Count aloud each line of rhythm. Observe the rests by saying "rest" on each beat of rest. Finally, count without saying the word "rest," but carefully include its correct duration.

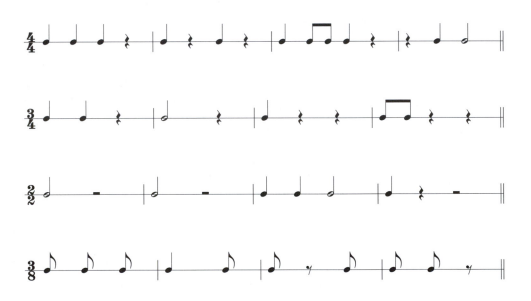

PRACTICE

Singing and Playing with Rests

Sing each line on one pitch, using the syllable "loo." Then play each line on a percussion instrument, on one key of a piano, or on one recorder note.

ANACRUSIS (UPBEAT)

Many songs and instrumental pieces begin with an incomplete measure called an *anacrusis* or *upbeat*. These unaccented notes can be illustrated through language and are shown below in examples of notation with lyrics. Observe that the first accented syllable in the lyrics is the first beat of the first complete measure of the song. The last measure combined with the anacrusis equals the correct number of beats for one complete measure.

BLUE HAWAIIAN SKY

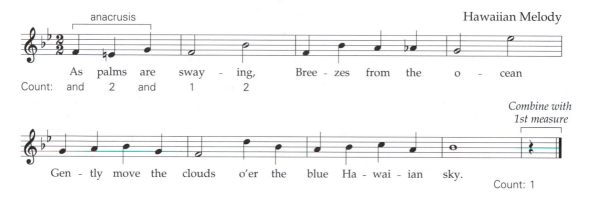

CANON

MUSICAL APPLICATION

Listening to the Anacrusis

Each of these musical excerpts begins with an anacrusis, or upbeat. Tap the rhythms before you listen, then as you listen.

FUGUE 11 in F MAJOR (R-18)
from *The Well-Tempered Clavier*, Book I

Johann Sebastian Bach
(Germany, 1685–1750)

Count: 3   1   2   3   1   2 & 3 &

FARANDOLE (R-19)
from *L'Arlésienne* Suite No. 2

Georges Bizet
(France, 1838–1875)

Count: &   1 & 2 &

FOURTH MOVEMENT (R-20)
from Symphony No. 40 in G Minor, K. 550

Wolfgang Amadeus Mozart
(Austria, 1756–1791)

1st violins

Count: &   1   &   2   &

TIES

A *tie* extends a note's duration with a curved line that connects horizontally two or more noteheads representing the same pitch. In performance, the first of the tied notes is articulated and the sound is continued through the duration of the second note. Sometimes, more than two notes are tied.

Here are some examples of tied notes and their durational equivalents.

Although the tie and the *slur* have a similar appearance, the slur is always between two notes of different pitches, whereas the tie is always between notes of identical pitch.

Tie

attack ⌣ hold

Slur

Play on one breath
or sing on one word

PRACTICE

Playing Ties

Play the following example with ties on one note of a keyboard. You should make a sound only on the first of the tied notes, then sustain the sound through the value of the note(s) to which it is tied. When you are counting, the numbers in parentheses are not articulated but are sustained.

1   2 - (3)   4   1   2 & 3 &- (4)   1- (2)   3   4 -   (1) & 2   3   Rest

Count, tap, then hum these examples with ties.

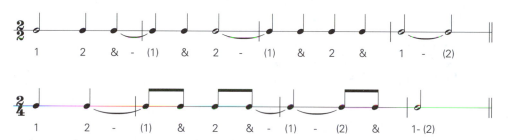

1   2   & - (1)   & 2   -   (1)   &   2   &   1   -   (2)

1   2   -   (1)   & 2   & - (1)   -   (2)   &   1- (2)

PRACTICE

Identifying Equivalent Values of Tied Notes

Write one note that is equivalent to each tied group.

Write the total number of beats indicated for each pair of tied notes.

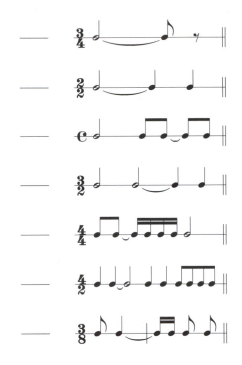

MUSICAL APPLICATION

Listening to Ties

Tap out the rhythm of each excerpt. Then listen to each one. Tap the excerpts again.

There is a strong accent on the first of the tied notes in this symphonic movement and in the Chopin waltz.

THIRD MOVEMENT (R-21)
from Symphony No. 40 in G Minor, K. 550

Wolfgang Amadeus Mozart
(Austria, 1756–1791)

VALSE, OP. 69, NO. 2 (R-22)

Frédéric Chopin
(Poland, 1810–1849)

PRACTICE

Singing Songs with Ties and Rests

SING NOEL

Liberian Round

SHE'LL BE COMIN' 'ROUND THE MOUNTAIN

U.S.A.

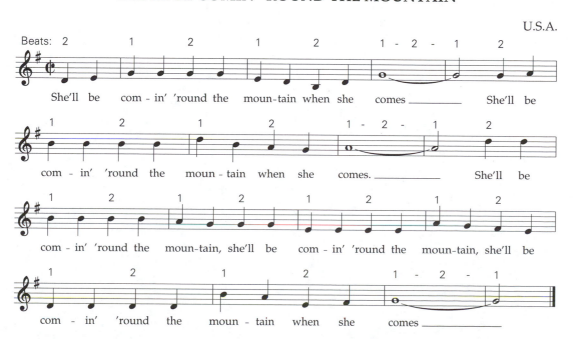

PRACTICE

Counting with Rests, Ties, and Anacrusis

Count aloud each example using numbers and syllables. Tap the beats with your foot. Then play each example on one key of a piano.

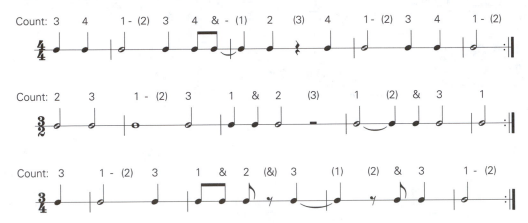

DOTTED NOTE AND REST VALUES

Rhythms are not always even with the beat. The symbols that represent uneven note values use dots beside the noteheads. A dot placed to the right side of a note or a rest adds half the duration of that note or rest to the note or rest. Division of a dotted note results in three equal parts, and subdivision results in six equal parts, as shown in the following chart.

dotted whole note	o·	equals	o	plus	𝅗𝅥
dotted half note	𝅗𝅥·	=	𝅗𝅥	+	♩
dotted quarter note	♩·	=	♩	+	♪
dotted eighth note	♪·	=	♪	+	♬
dotted sixteenth note	𝅘𝅥𝅯·	=	𝅘𝅥𝅯	+	𝅘𝅥𝅰
dotted 32nd note	𝅘𝅥𝅰·	=	𝅘𝅥𝅰	+	𝅘𝅥𝅱

Note	Division	Subdivision

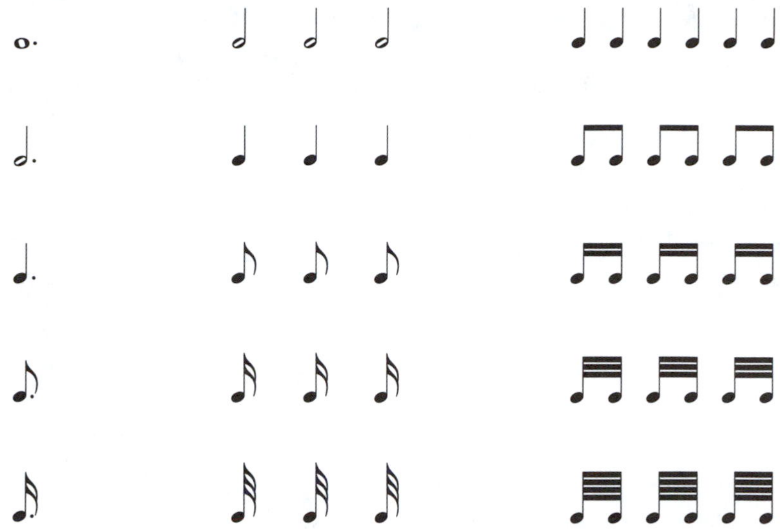

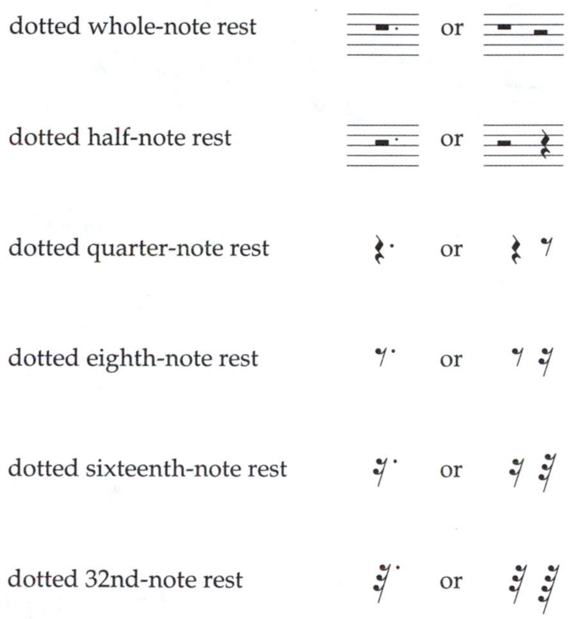

dotted whole-note rest 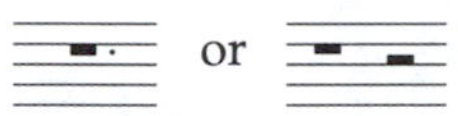

dotted half-note rest 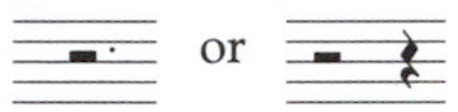

dotted quarter-note rest 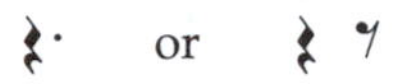

dotted eighth-note rest 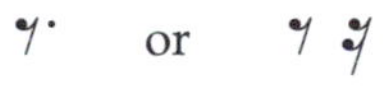

dotted sixteenth-note rest 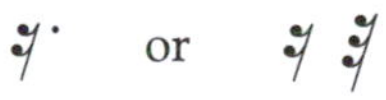

dotted 32nd-note rest 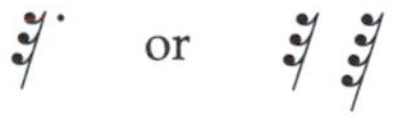

The Dotted Half Note

The *dotted half note* is sustained for three beats in simple meters.

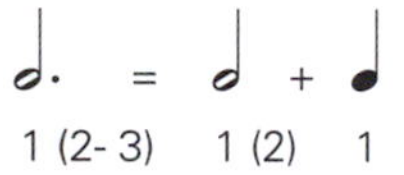

Clap or tap these exercises that use the dotted half note.

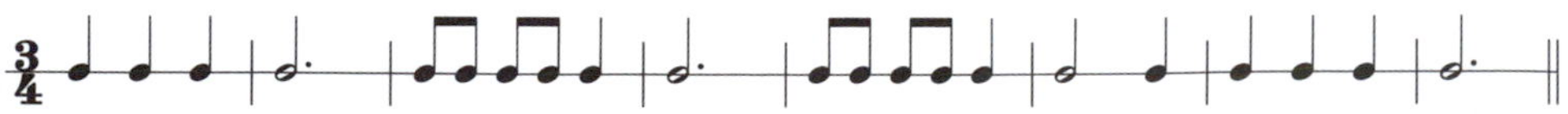

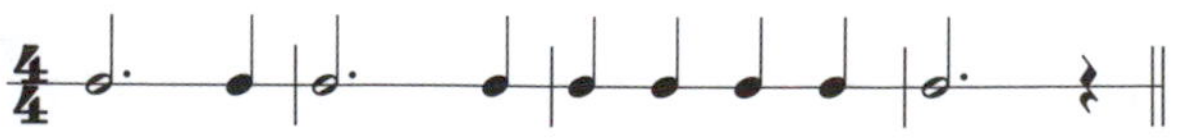

MUSICAL APPLICATION

Singing Songs with Dotted Half Notes

Practice reading the dotted half note in these songs.

THE SIDEWALKS OF NEW YORK

James W. Blake
(United States, 1862–1935)

Charles B. Lawlor
(United States, 1852–1925)

MY HAT

German Folk Song

OLD SMOKY

American Ballad

The Dotted-Quarter-Note–Eighth-Note Pattern

The dotted quarter note followed by an eighth note—♩. ♪ —and the less common reversed pattern—♪ ♩. —are found in the rhythms of Western cultures from stately processionals to Latin dances. You can learn to perform the dotted quarter note in these derivative exercises that begin with the basic beat.

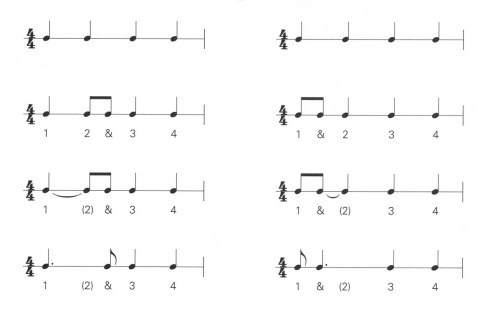

PRACTICE

Counting Dotted-Quarter-Note–Eighth-Note Patterns

Practice counting the dotted-quarter-note–eighth-note patterns in these examples. Remember, the dot is always counted as a number, and the second half of that number's beat (the eighth note) is counted with the word "and."

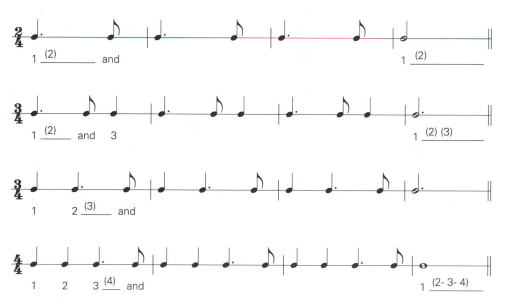

MUSICAL APPLICATION

Singing the Dotted-Quarter-Note–Eighth-Note Pattern

With your instructor's assistance, sing these songs that include dotted-quarter-note–eighth-note rhythms. Then count the rhythms aloud.

AMERICA THE BEAUTIFUL
(excerpt)

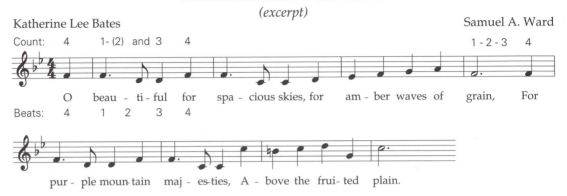

AULD LANG SYNE
(excerpt)

HARU GA KITA

CRAWDAD

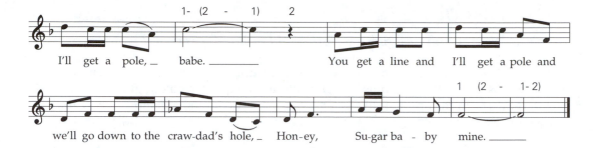

I'll get a pole, _ babe. _ You get a line and I'll get a pole and

we'll go down to the craw-dad's hole, _ Hon-ey, Su-gar ba - by mine. _

MUSICAL APPLICATION

Listening to Dotted-Quarter-Note–Eighth-Note Patterns

Listen to dotted-quarter-note–eighth-note rhythms in these musical works.
Then count the rhythm aloud, tapping the beat with your hand.

WALTZ IN A-FLAT MAJOR, OP. 39, NO. 15 (R-23)
(excerpt)

Johannes Brahms
(Germany, 1833–1897)

FAR ABOVE CAYUGA'S WATERS
Cornell University Alma Mater

Wilmot Smith
Archibold Croswell

Far a-bove Cay - u - ga's wa-ters, With its waves of blue, Stands our no - ble

al - ma ma - ter, Glo - ri-ous to view. Lift the cho - rus, speed it on-ward,

Loud her prai-ses tell. Hail to thee, our al - ma ma-ter, Hail to thee, Cor - nell.

PRACTICE

Writing Dotted-Quarter-Note–Eighth-Note Patterns

Rewrite each four-measure line to create dotted-quarter-note–eighth-note rhythms from either two quarter-note patterns or a quarter-note–eighth-note pattern. Perform the original rhythm and your new rhythm on a piano key, a drum, or one recorder note.

The Dotted-Eighth-Note–Sixteenth-Note Pattern

The dotted eighth followed by a sixteenth note—♪. ♬—and the reverse pattern—♬. —are also common in Western rhythm. The derivations for these patterns are shown below. Study the examples, and tap out the four lines of each one in succession to feel the rhythm against the beats you tap with your foot.

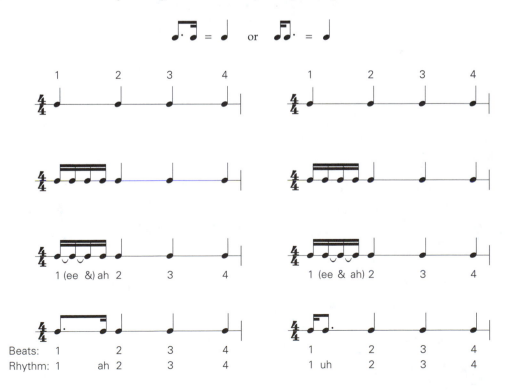

PRACTICE

Counting the Dotted-Eighth-Note–Sixteenth-Note Pattern

Count aloud each four-measure phrase. Then "remove" the dots and make each dotted pattern into evenly divided eighth-note groups. Practice each line both ways several times.

PRACTICE

Playing the Dotted-Eighth-Note–Sixteenth-Note Pattern

Play each line on a percussion instrument, a piano key, or a recorder note.

MUSICAL APPLICATION

Singing Songs with Dotted-Eighth-Note–Sixteenth-Note Patterns

Sing these songs, observing the dotted-eighth-note–sixteenth-note patterns.
Which songs include the ♪. ♪ pattern? Which songs have the ♪ ♪. pattern?

THE BATTLE HYMN OF THE REPUBLIC
(excerpt)

Julia Ward Howe   William Steffe

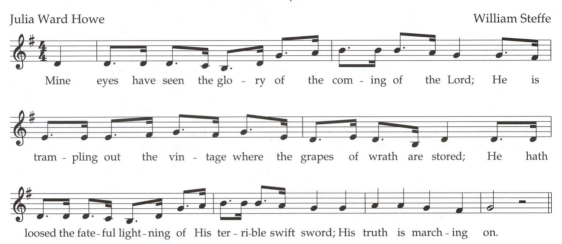

Mine eyes have seen the glo - ry of the com - ing of the Lord; He is

tram - pling out the vin - tage where the grapes of wrath are stored; He hath

loosed the fate - ful light - ning of His ter - ri-ble swift sword; His truth is march - ing on.

MICHAEL, ROW THE BOAT ASHORE

African-American Spiritual

Mich - ael, row - the boat a - shore, *Hal - le - lu - - jah!* Mich - ael,

row the boat a - shore, *Hal - le - lu - - jah!*

EZEK'EL SAW THE WHEEL

Black-American Spiritual

E - ze-k'el saw the wheel! 'Way up in the mid-dle o' the air, E -

ze - k'el saw the wheel! 'Way in the mid-dle o' the air, The

big wheel moved by Faith, The Lit - tle Wheel moved by the Grace o' God, A

wheel   in   a   wheel ____   'Way   in the mid-dle o' the   air.

KUM BA YAH

Black-American

Kum ba yah, my Lord, Kum ba yah.   Kum ba yah, my Lord, Kum ba yah.   Kum ba

yah, my Lord, Kum ba yah,   Oh,   Lord... ____   Kum ba yah.

WORRIED MAN

U.S.A.

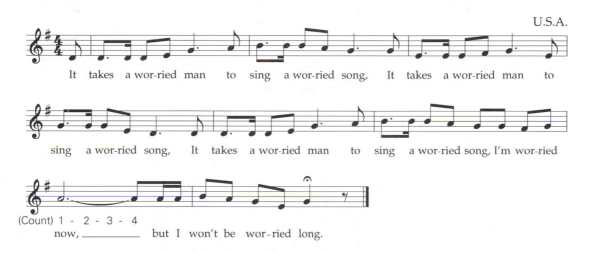

It takes a wor-ried man   to   sing a wor-ried song,   It   takes a wor-ried man   to

sing   a wor-ried song,   It   takes a wor-ried man   to   sing   a wor-ried song, I'm wor-ried

(Count) 1 - 2 - 3 - 4

now, _____ but I won't be wor-ried long.

MUSICAL APPLICATION

Listening to the Dotted-Eighth-Note–Sixteenth-Note Pattern

Count aloud the rhythm of each piece, tapping the beats with your hand. Then hum the excerpts with your instructor's assistance. Follow the scores as you listen.

SECOND MOVEMENT (R-24)
from Symphony No. 5 *(From the New World)* in E Minor
(excerpt)

Antonín Dvořák
(Bohemia, 1841–1904)

MINUET IN G (R-25)

Ludwig van Beethoven
(Germany, 1770–1827)

PRELUDE IN C MINOR, OP. 28, NO. 20 (R-26)

Frédéric Chopin
(Poland, 1810–1849)

TAPS
(Bugle Call)

FOURTH MOVEMENT (R-27)
from Quintet for Clarinet and Strings in A Major

Wolfgang Amadeus Mozart
(Austria, 1756–1791)

NORWEGIAN DANCE

Edvard Grieg
(Norway, 1843–1907)

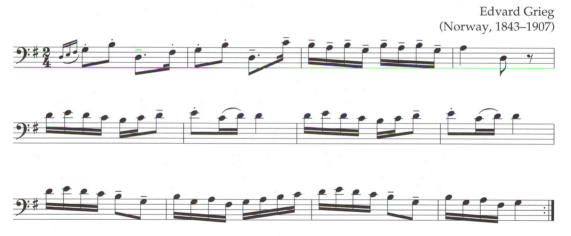

TRIPLETS AND BORROWED DIVISION

In simple meters, we usually divide and subdivide beats into two equal parts:

When we divide a beat into three equal parts in simple meter, we create a *triplet*; we show the division with the number 3 over the group of notes. This placement of three notes normally performed in the time of two is called a *borrowed division.* If there is no beam joining the notes, a bracket is used to include the notes in the triplet.

Tap the following measures, making sure that you perform the triplets evenly. Count as you tap.

MUSICAL APPLICATION

Singing Triplets

Identify the triplet patterns in the following song. Write the counting numbers over the notes; then sing the song.

NINE HUNDRED MILES

Traditional

I am walk - in' down the track, I got tears _____ in my eyes,

Try-in' to read a let - ter from my home.   *Chorus*   If that train runs me right, I'll be

home Sat-ur-day night, For I'm nine hun-dred miles _ from _ home,   And I

hate to hear that lone-some whis-tle blow.

MUSICAL APPLICATION

Listening to Triplets

Listen to the triplet figures in each excerpt.

HABAÑERA (R-28)

Alexis Chabrier
(France, 1841–1894)

PRELUDE, OP. 28, NO. 14

Frédéric Chopin
(Poland, 1810–1849)

ERLKÖNIG (R-29)

Franz Schubert
(Germany, 1797–1828)

HABANERA
from *Carmen*

Georges Bizet
(France, 1838–1875)

EXPRESSION MARKINGS

Although we are focusing on reading rhythm notation, we must keep in mind that notation serves only as a guide for the performer. The expressive qualities in music represent that part of the art that cannot be indicated by written notation alone. The performer brings the musical score to life with color and expression. Included in expressive qualities are *tempo* and *dynamics*—the *pace of the beats* in a musical work and the *volume* used in its presentation. Over the centuries, composers and musicians have employed generally agreed-upon markings that assist the performer in presenting music with the tempo and dynamics desired by the composer.

Tempo

The first composer to give precise indications of intended tempi for his compositions was Beethoven. An apparatus called the metronome, which is used to indicate the tempo of a piece, was constructed by Johannes Maelzel in 1816. Modern metronomes range from the simple windup types to electric ones with flashing lights indicating the beats. Many musical works have an *M.M.* ("Maelzel's Metronome") marking at the beginning of the score to indicate the tempo, or beats per minute. The following list shows the common tempo terms and their metronome markings for a quarter-note beat in $\frac{4}{4}$.

Largo (42–66)—very slow
Lento (52–108)—very slow
Adagio (50–76)—slowly, leisurely
Andante (56–88)—moderately
Moderato (66–126)—moderately

Allegro (84–144)—fast, lively
Vivace (80–160)—animated, lively
Presto (100–152)—very rapidly
Prestissimo (120–180)—extremely fast

Additional terms related to tempo are

Accelerando (*accel.*)—gradually increasing tempo
A tempo—return to original tempo
Ritardando (*rit.*)—gradually slower and slower
Ritenuto (*riten.*)—immediately slowing in tempo
Rubato—a deliberate unsteadiness of tempo

Dynamics

The volume of a sound depends on the strength of the vibration that produces it. The stronger the stimulation, the louder the sound, and vice versa. When a piano key is struck, a louder or softer sound is produced according to the energy of the stroke. Dynamic markings are used by composers to assist performers in choosing the appropriate volume in the range from very soft to very loud sounds. These marks are usually written under the staff. Here is a list of commonly used dynamic markings.

fff—*molto fortissimo* (extremely loud)
ff—*fortissimo* (very loud)
f—*forte* (loud)
mf—*mezzo forte* (fairly loud)

mp—*mezzo piano* (fairly soft)
p—*piano* (soft)
pp—*pianissimo* (very soft)
ppp—*molto pianissimo* (extremely soft)

$\prec$ *Crescendo* (*cresc.*)—gradually louder
$\succ$ *Decrescendo* (*decresc.*)—gradually softer
$\succ$ *Diminuendo* (*dim., dimin.*)—gradually softer

Style and Expression

A manner or style of performance is suggested by these terms:

Animato—animatedly
Cantabile—in a singing style
Dolce—sweetly
Giocoso—joyfully
Grazioso—gracefully
Legato—smoothly, connected

Maestoso—majestically
Sforzando—a strong accent
Sostenuto—sustained
Staccato—short, detached
Tenuto—sustain for full value

Additional directive terms are

Fermata (⌢)—hold or pause
Meno—less
Molto—much
Più, peu—more
Poco—little

PRACTICE

Working with Tempo and Dynamics

Go back to the rhythm exercises on page 61. Try them with different metronome markings; then put in selected dynamic markings. Perform them according to both your metronome and your dynamic markings.

PRACTICE

Creating and Performing Eight-Measure Phrases

A musical *phrase* is comparable to a clause in language; it conveys part of a complete thought that contributes to a composition. Your assignment here is to create an eight-measure phrase in each meter indicated below. You may perform your phrases as solos or in a group by clapping or playing on percussion instruments as you tap your feet on the beats.

1. Use these notes and rests in any combinations:

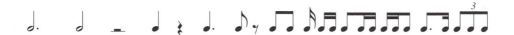

2. In your first efforts, use rests only at the ends of measures, preferably at the end of the last measure. Use ties sparingly.
3. Use dynamic markings.
4. Perform your phrases at various tempi yourself; then decide on M.M. markings.

$\frac{3}{2}$ _____

$\frac{3}{4}$ _____

¢ _____

$\frac{3}{8}$ _____

$\frac{4}{4}$ _____

MUSICAL APPLICATION

Listening to Simple Meters, Tempi, and Dynamics

Listen carefully as each excerpt is performed. Use a metronome to determine the tempo at which the work is played. How does the tempo affect the overall impression of the work? What are the dynamic indications in these examples?

TROUT QUINTET, OP. 114 (R-30)

Franz Schubert
(Austria, 1797–1828)

THE VIENNESE MUSICAL CLOCK (R-31)
from the *Háry János* Suite

Zoltán Kodály
(Hungary, 1882–1967)

FIRST MOVEMENT (R-32)
from *Brandenburg Concerto No. 5*

Johann Sebastian Bach
(Germany, 1685–1750)

THOUSAND AND ONE NIGHTS, OP. 346

Johann Strauss
(Austria, 1825–1899)

SECOND MOVEMENT (R-33)
from Symphony No. 5

Ludwig van Beethoven
(Germany, 1770–1827)

MEIN HERR MARQUIS
from *Die Fledermaus*

Johann Strauss
(Austria, 1825–1899)

REVIEW

Counting and Singing in Simple Meters

Tap the beats and count the rhythm for each song before you sing it with your group. Which songs begin with upbeats?

THE GLENDY BURK
(excerpt)

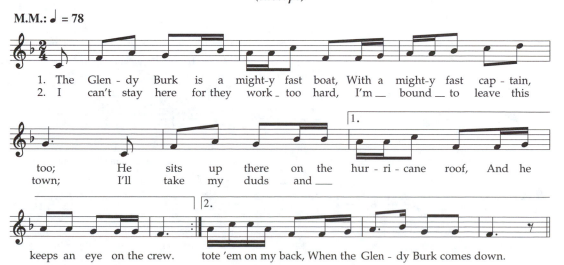

See Appendix C for help with lines two and three.

DONA NOBIS PACEM
(Grant Us Peace)

Do - na   no - bis   pa - cem, pa - cem,   do - na __

no - bis pa - - cem.

ODE TO JOY
from Symphony No. 9 in D Major
(excerpt)

Ludwig van Beethoven
(Germany, 1770–1827)

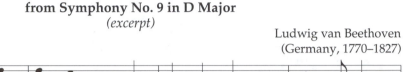

Freud - e, schoen - er Goet - ter - funk - en, Toch - ter aus E - ly - si - um,
froy deh shuu - nehr guu - tehr - foon - ken tahk - tehr aoos aye - lee - see-oom,

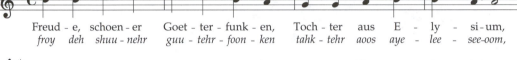

Wir be - tre - ten feu - er - trunk - en. Himm - li - sche, dein Heil - ig - tum!
veer bee - tray - tehn foy - er - troon - kehn him - lih - sheh dine hy - lihg - toom!

English Version (Henry Van Dyke):

Joyful, joyful, <u>we</u> adore thee,
<u>God</u> of glory, <u>Lord</u> of love;
<u>Hearts</u> unfold like <u>flow</u>'rs before thee,
Op'ning to the <u>sun</u> above.

BLACK IS THE COLOR OF MY TRUE LOVE'S HAIR

M.M.: ♩ = 60

Appalachian Folk Song

1. Black black, black is the col - or of my true love's hair. Those
2. How I love my __ love and well she knows, __ I

lips are like some ros - y fair; The pur - est __ eyes and the
love the grass where-on she goes; When she on __ earth no __

neat - est __ hands, I love the grass where - on she stands.
more __ I __ see, My life will quick - ly o - ver be.

WAYFARING STRANGER
(excerpt)

Southern White Spiritual
U.S.A.

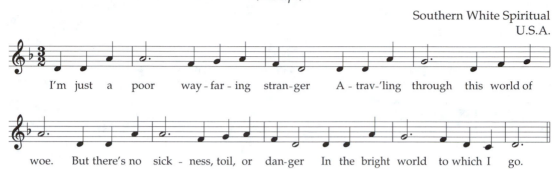

I'm just a poor way-far-ing stran-ger A-trav-'ling through this world of

woe. But there's no sick-ness, toil, or dan-ger In the bright world to which I go.

AMAZING GRACE

John Newton
(England, 1725–1807)

American Folk Hymn

M.M.: ♩ = 76

A - ma - zing _ grace, how sweet the sound, That saved a ____

wretch like me: _____ I once was lost but

now am __ found, was blind but __ now I see. _____

SHALOM, CHAVERIM

Israeli Round

Sha - lom, cha-ve-rim! Sha - lom cha-ve-rim! Sha - lom, sha - lom! Le -

hit - ra - ot, le - hit - ra - ot, Sha - lom, sha - lom!

English Text:

Farewell, good friends, Farewell, good friends,
Farewell, farewell!
Till we meet again, till we meet again,
Farewell, farewell!

I'VE BEEN WORKING ON THE RAILROAD

OLD BIRD, OLD BIRD

Translation:

Old bird, old bird—you old green bird,
Do not sit down on the noktu bush.
If the noktu flowers fall on the ground,
Then the Jonman will go
Crying away,
Crying away.

TOEMBAI

M.M.: ♩ = 116

Israeli Round

① Toem - bai, toem - bai, toem - bai, toem - bai, toem - bai, toem - bai, toem - bai.

② Tra la la, la la la la la, La la la la la la.

③ Tra la la la la, La la la la la, La la la la la, la.

RING, RING THE BANJO

M.M.: ♩ = 96

Stephen Foster
(United States, 1826–1864)

Beats: 1   2   1   2   1   2

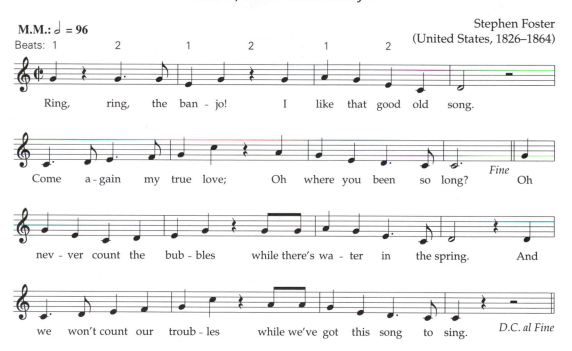

Ring, ring, the ban - jo! I like that good old song.

Come a - gain my true love; Oh where you been so long? *Fine* Oh

nev - ver count the bub - bles while there's wa - ter in the spring. And

we won't count our troub - les while we've got this song to sing. *D.C. al Fine*

ZUM GALI GALI

REVIEW OF TERMS

Define each term. Where appropriate, draw, notate, or present in a musical context to demonstrate your understanding.

1. rest
2. anacrusis
3. upbeat
4. tie
5. dotted note
6. dotted rest
7. division of dotted note
8. subdivision of dotted note
9. triplet
10. borrowed division
11. expressive markings
12. tempo
13. dynamics
14. phrase
15. fermata
16. meno
17. molto
18. più
19. poco

WORKSHEET
Chapter 3 Review

1. Write a rest that is equivalent to each note.

♩. _____   ♪ _____

♪ _____   o· _____

♩. _____   ♪ _____

2. Place each rest that you drew in exercise 1 on the staff correctly.

3. What is an anacrusis (also called an upbeat)? Give two examples in notation.

4. Give the English definitions for these terms related to tempo.

   presto _____

   adagio _____

   lento _____

   allegro _____

   vivace _____

   largo _____

   prestissimo _____

   andante _____

   accelerando _____

   rubato _____

   ritenuto _____

   ritardando _____

   a tempo _____

5. What symbols are used to indicate these degrees of volume?

   gradually softer _____   soft _____

   very soft _____   extremely soft _____

   extremely loud _____   very loud _____

   fairly loud _____   loud _____

   gradually louder _____

6. What is a metronome? Which composer was the first to indicate an appropriate tempo for each composition? What does *M.M.* mean?

7. Count this rhythmic exercise correctly, making a sound only on the first note of a tied group and sustaining the sound through the value of the note(s) to which it is tied.

8. Add the last line in this group to show the derivation of the dotted-quarter-note–eighth-note pattern.

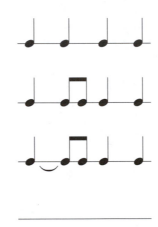

9. Add the last line in this group to show the derivation of the dotted-eighth-note–sixteenth-note pattern.

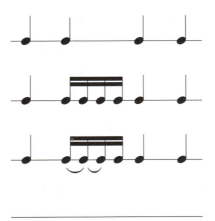

10. Add beams to create the correct number of beats per measure.

11. How much duration is added to a note by a dot?

12. Add dots to create the correct number of beats per measure.

13. Notate each rhythm as your instructor performs it.

a. $\frac{3}{4}$ _____

b. $\frac{3}{8}$ _____

c. $\mathtext{¢}$ _____

d. $\frac{2}{2}$ _____

e. $\frac{4}{4}$ _____

f. $\frac{3}{4}$ _____

g. $\mathtext{C}$ _____

14. Complete this chart showing the three notes that constitute each division of the dotted note and the six notes that make up its subdivisions.

Dotted Note	Division	Subdivision
𝅝·		
𝅗𝅥·		
♩·		
♪·		
𝅘𝅥𝅯·		

15. Write the counting numbers under the notation. Tap out the rhythm for your instructor.

(continued)

16. Write the Italian musical terms that mean

    animatedly _____

    in a singing style _____

    sweetly _____

    joyfully _____

    gracefully _____

    smoothly, connected _____

    majestically _____

    a strong accent _____

    sustained _____

    short, detached _____

    sustain for full value _____

17. What does each directive term mean?

    fermata _____

    meno _____

    molto _____

    più, peu _____

    poco _____

CHAPTER PROJECTS

1. Create an eight-measure exercise in simple meter made up of any combinations of these notes:

   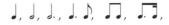

   and rests:

   𝄽   𝄼

   Include tempo and dynamic markings. Perform it as a soloist or with a group of classmates.

2. In your library, locate a book of carols or a collection of folk songs. Find examples of simple meters and practice counting aloud some of the songs.

3. Learn the basic conducting patterns for these meters: $\frac{2}{2}$, $\frac{2}{4}$, $\frac{3}{2}$, $\frac{3}{4}$, $\frac{4}{4}$, ¢. Conduct one of the songs in "Singing in Simple Meters," p. 71. (See Appendix B.)

4. Notate the rhythm of your school's alma mater.

5. Listen to these works while following their scores; then answer the questions that follow.

   Ludwig van Beethoven: String Quartet, Op. 18, No. 1, First Movement

   Johannes Brahms: Ballade, Op. 118, No. 3

   Frederic Chopin: Mazurka, Op. 17, No. 2

   a. What is the meter of each piece?

   b. What is its tempo or M.M.?

   c. Which one(s) begin(s) with an anacrusis?

   d. What dynamic levels are indicated? Do they change as the piece is performed? Often?

6. With a partner, tap out the rhythm of this keyboard piece, one person performing the right-hand part, the other performing the left-hand part.

Major Scales and Keys

SCALES

In Chapters 4 and 5, you will learn how music is constructed from a series of pitches that are arranged in a specific order called a *scale.* There are many scales in use globally, but the two that have dominated Western culture since about 1600 are called the *major* and the *minor* scales. (Scales in use during the Medieval and Renaissance periods are called church modes and are discussed later in this text.)

The Octave

We can begin our study of scales by examining the *octave.* An octave is the distance between a given pitch and the one produced by a vibration that is twice the speed of the first. The two pitches have the same letter name, and you can locate an octave on a keyboard very quickly. Start by playing middle C; then play the C above middle C. The distance between the two notes is an octave, and the number of keys embraced is thirteen, including both C's. You can locate other octaves on your keyboard by following the same procedure: Look for two keys with the same letter name that embrace a distance of thirteen keys.

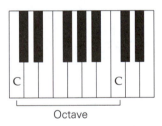

Octave

The Chromatic Scale

If we play every key in an octave from 1 to 13, we have played the *chromatic scale,* in which the distance from note to note is a half step.

C C♯/D♭ D D♯/E♭ E F F♯/G♭ G G♯/A♭ A A♯/B♭ B C
1 2 3 4 5 6 7 8 9 10 11 12 13

The ascending chromatic scale is notated with sharps; the descending chromatic scale is notated with flats. Note that E–F and B–C are notated as natural notes. Incorrect spellings would be F♭–F or E–E♯, and C♭–C or B–B♯.

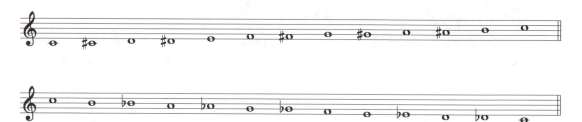

The Major Scale, Pitch Classes, Diatonic

The *major scale*, like the chromatic scale, embraces an octave. However, it does not include all thirteen notes of the octave but, rather, the seven *pitch classes* of a key, with a specific linear arrangement of two half steps and five whole steps. Therefore, it is called a *diatonic* scale, meaning that it does not use only half steps. The tonic, or first note of the scale, is labeled with the scale-degree number 1 and appears again as number 8. A major scale can begin on any pitch and always appears with this pattern of whole steps and half steps:

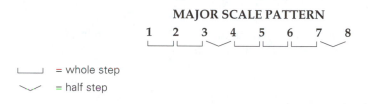

The easiest major scale to play on the keyboard is the C major scale **(R-60)**, which employs only white keys. The major scale can be played or sung with either ascending or descending notes.

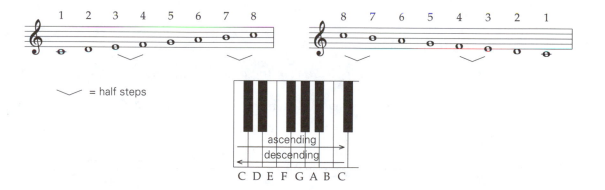

Key, Tonic

A song built from notes of the C major scale is *in the key of C major.* A song in the key of C major is made up of tones from the C scale placed in an order desired by the composer. The pitch, or tone, receiving the most emphasis throughout the song and almost always appearing as the song's final note is C. This most prominent tone is referred to as the *tonic,* or home note. In the key of D major, the most prominent tone is D; in the key of E major, the most prominent tone is E; and so on.

Melodic Syllable Names: Tonic Sol-Fa

Each note of a scale is assigned a melodic syllable name to aid in sight-reading melodies based on the scale. One system that uses these syllables to sing the notes of a melody is called *tonic sol-fa*. In major scales, the order of the syllables is

1 2 3 4 5 6 7 8

(1)

do re mi fa sol la ti do

The distance from *do* (1) to *do* (8) is an octave.

In a melody, the notes of a scale are used to create a melodic contour, or definitive shape of a tune. Can you identify the songs in which these melodies appear? Follow the syllables to locate the notes on a keyboard. *Do* (1) is middle C.

*do do sol sol la la sol*_____

*sol mi do(1) mi sol do (8)*_____

*mi re do mi re do sol fa fa mi sol fa fa mi*_____

Scale-Degree Names

Just as the first degree of a scale is known as the tonic, the other pitches in a scale have degree names, too. These names show the relationship of a given pitch to its tonic.

SCALE DEGREE NAMES IN C MAJOR

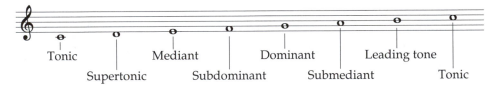

Tonic   Mediant   Dominant   Leading tone

Supertonic   Subdominant   Submediant   Tonic

PRACTICE

Notating the C Major Scale, Ascending and Descending

Notate the C major scale above its letters, numbers, and syllables.

Ascending scale:

	C	D	E	F	G	A	B	C
	1	2	3	4	5	6	7	8
	Do	Re	Mi	Fa	Sol	Re	Ti	Do

Descending scale:

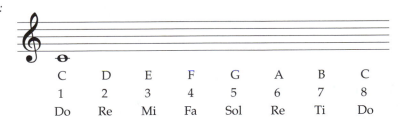

	C	B	A	G	F	E	D	C
	8	7	6	5	4	3	2	1
	Do	Ti	La	Sol	Fa	Mi	Re	Do

PRACTICE

Identifying Pitches in C Major with Letter Names, Scale Numbers, and Melodic Syllables

Write the letter names, scale numbers, and melodic syllables over the notes of this song in the key of C major. Sing it with your class.

WHEN THE SAINTS GO MARCHING IN

Black-American Spiritual

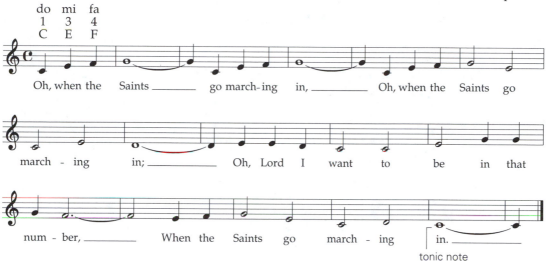

The Key of G Major and Movable *Do*

Now let's write a major scale beginning on G. There are eight pitches in the scale, and the beginning and ending letters are the same, since the scale embraces an octave and must include all the letters of the musical alphabet. Observe that the syllable *do* is assigned to the first note of the scale in the tonic *sol-fa* system and is called *movable do*. C is *do* in the C major scale; G is *do* in the G major scale; and so on.

Letters:	G	A	B	C	D	E	F	G
Numbers:	1	2	3	4	5	6	7	8
Melodic Syllables:	*do*	*re*	*mi*	*fa*	*sol*	*la*	*ti*	*do*

C major is the only major scale using only the white keys. Other major keys make use of black keys. To understand which black key (or keys) is needed in G major, use the procedure outlined below. This procedure can be applied to the writing of any major scale, beginning on any key on your keyboard.

PROCEDURE FOR CREATING A MAJOR SCALE ON G

In a major key, all steps should be whole steps except 3–4 and 7–8.

1. Move from white key to white key, left to right, to check your scale. Use a black key only where needed to create the necessary patterns of whole steps and half steps.
2. We see that G–A and A–B are whole steps on the white keys.
3. B–C is a half step between 3 and 4 and is correctly placed.

4. C–D and D–E are whole steps, also correctly placed on the white keys.

5. But we're supposed to have a whole step between 6 and 7. If we remain on the white keys, 6–7 will be a half step. We can create the required whole step here by raising the F to an F-sharp.* Moving from F-sharp to G also creates the half step we need in moving from 7 to 8.

Our corrected G major scale looks like this (⌄ = half step):

THE G MAJOR SCALE

G   A   B   C   D   E   F♯   G
1   2   3 ⌄ 4   5   6   7   ⌄ 8
do   re   mi ⌄ fa   sol la   ti ⌄ do

PRACTICE

Locating the Notes of the G Major Scale on a Keyboard

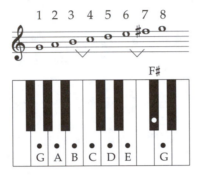

Key Signature

The notation for a song in G major will include a sharp sign (♯) on the F line at the beginning of the score, right after the clef sign. This ♯, or *key signature*, tells the performer that all F's in the song will be sharped. Thus, sharp signs will not appear before each F in the song.

The key signature for the key of G major in the treble clef looks like this:

PRACTICE

*Writing Note Names, Scale Numbers,
and Melodic Syllables in G Major*

Identify the notes of this song using the three systems. Then sing the song with your classmates. (Note the order of appearance at the beginning of a musical score from left to right: clef sign, key signature, time signature.)

---

*Each scale must comprise all the letter names of the musical alphabet. Thus, we cannot move to G-flat. That would create a scale with no F's and two G's—a misspelling.

CHATTER WITH THE ANGELS

American Spiritual

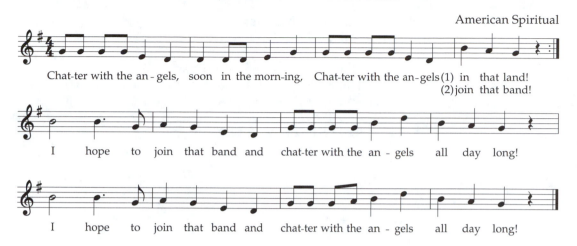

Chat-ter with the an-gels, soon in the morn-ing, Chat-ter with the an-gels(1) in that land!
(2)join that band!

I hope to join that band and chat-ter with the an-gels all day long!

I hope to join that band and chat-ter with the an-gels all day long!

RANGE OF THE SONG S PITCHES

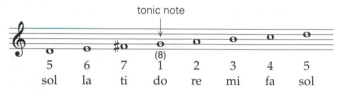

5	6	7	1	2	3	4	5
sol	la	ti	do	re	mi	fa	sol

The F Major Scale

The F major scale includes these letter names and the numbers and melodic sylla-bles associated with them. The scale includes one accidental, B-flat.

F	G	A	B♭	C	D	E	F
1	2	3	4	5	6	7	8
do	*re*	*mi*	*fa*	*sol*	*la*	*ti*	*do*

↑   ↑

tonic note   dominant note

Use your keyboard to see why the B-flat is needed to create a half step between 3 and 4 and the required whole step between 4 and 5. The E–F, or 7–8 of the scale, is a half step on the white keys.

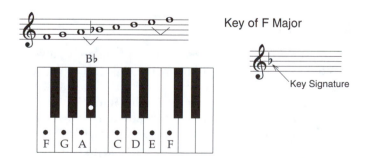

Key of F Major

Key Signature

PRACTICE

*Identifying Note Names, Scale Numbers,
and Melodic Syllables in F Major*

Write the letter names, scale numbers, and melodic syllables over the notes of this song in the key of F major. (Note that the song's range includes pitches from two consecutive F major scales.) Then sing it with your class.

RED RIVER VALLEY

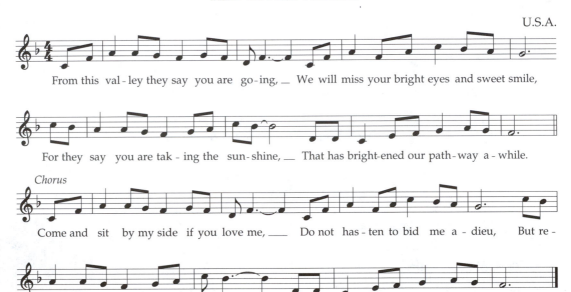

RANGE OF THE SONG'S PITCHES

MAJOR KEY SIGNATURES

The Circle of Fifths, Major Keys

You have studied the C, G, and F major keys. There are twelve other major keys, each with its own key signature. To make the task of learning these keys easier, a visual aid called the *circle of fifths* is invaluable. The key of C major, which has neither sharps nor flats, is at the top of the circle. Sharp keys, which employ from one to seven sharps in their signatures, are shown moving clockwise from C. Flat keys, which employ from one to seven flats, are shown moving counterclockwise from C. *Enharmonic keys,* which have different signatures but sound alike, are shown overlapping at the bottom of the circle.

How to Locate Key Names for Keys with Sharps   The key names moving successively from C in either direction are seven half steps, or a *perfect fifth,* apart. For example, moving a perfect fifth *up* the keyboard from C to locate the tonic of the key with one sharp, we arrive at G. Moving up the keyboard a fifth from G, we arrive at D, the name of the key with two sharps.

How to Locate Key Names for Keys with Flats   Moving a perfect fifth *down* the keyboard from C to locate the tonic of the key with one flat, we arrive at F. Moving down a perfect fifth from F, we arrive at B♭, the name of the key with two flats. Keys with two or more flats in their signatures include the flat symbol, ♭, and the word "flat" in their names—for example, B♭, E♭, A♭, D♭.

THE CIRCLE OF FIFTHS, MAJOR KEYS

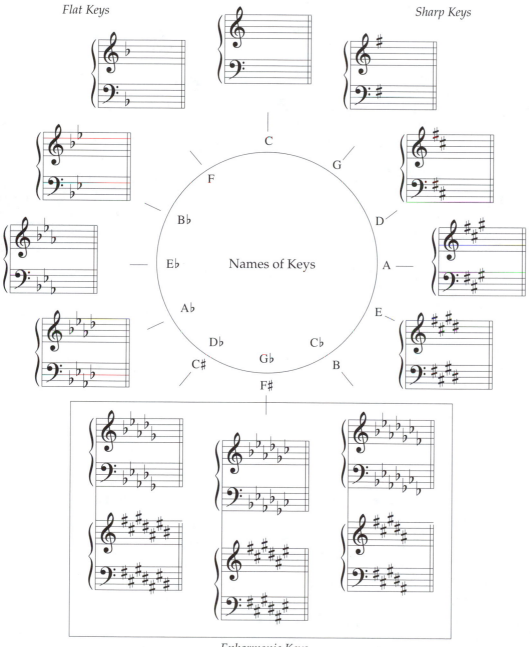

Enharmonic Keys

PRACTICE

Identifying Key Names from Key Signatures

When you see a major key signature and want to know the name of the key, there is another way to arrive at the answer. In keys with sharps, the last sharp to the right in the signature is designated *ti*, or the seventh degree of the scale. One half step *up* from *ti* (7) is *do* (8), or the first degree of the scale associated with the key signature, and thus its name. To identify the key name from a signature with flats, designate the last flat to the right as *fa*, or the fourth degree of the scale. Move scalewise *down* to *do* (1) and you have reached the letter name of the key associated with the signature. Another way to identify the tonic of flat major keys (except F major) is to designate the next-to-the-last flat as *do*. Examples are shown below.

1. The last sharp is *ti* or 7:

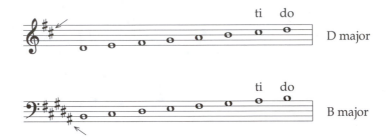

2. The last flat is *fa* or 4:

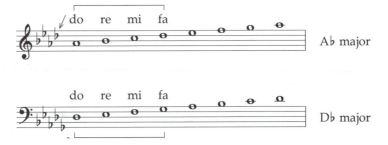

3. The next-to-the last flat is *do*, or 1:

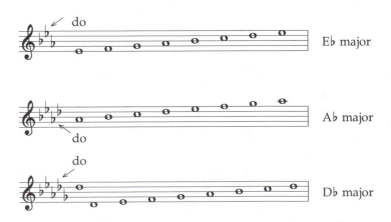

Major Scales with Sharps

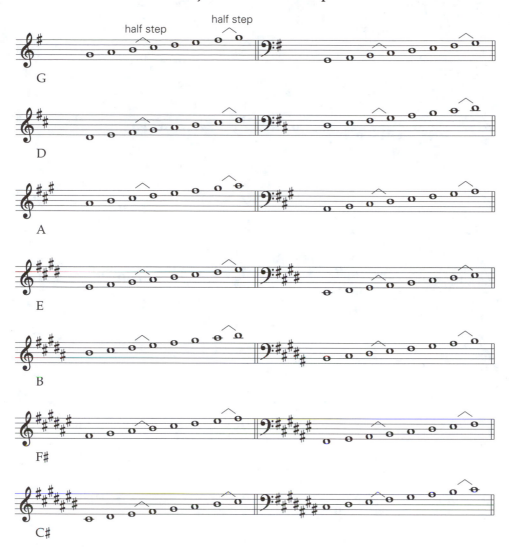

Major Scales with Flats

PRACTICE

Placing Key Signatures on the Staff

On the blank staves, copy each key signature, observing carefully the placement of the flats and sharps around lines or between lines. Write the letter name of the major key associated with each signature in the blank between the staves.

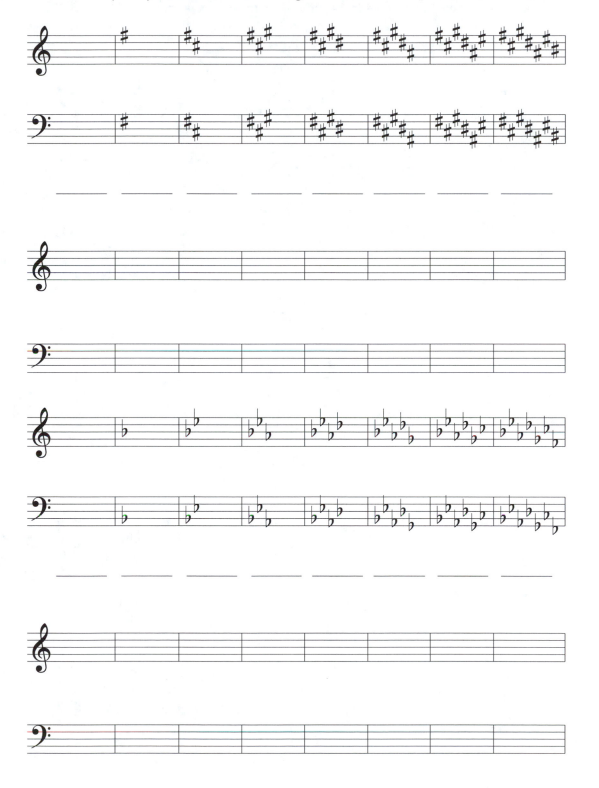

PRACTICE

Writing Major Scales;
Identifying Scale Notes on a Keyboard

Notate the major scales that correspond to the key signatures on the staves. Then write the scale-degree numbers 1–8 on the keyboard shown to the right of each scale. Where black keys are needed, write the numbers above the keys.

Major Key Name

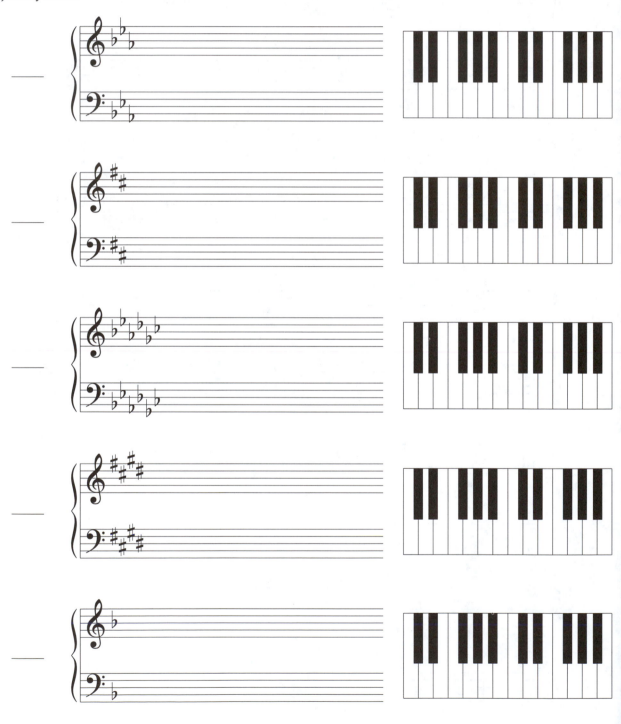

Major Key Name

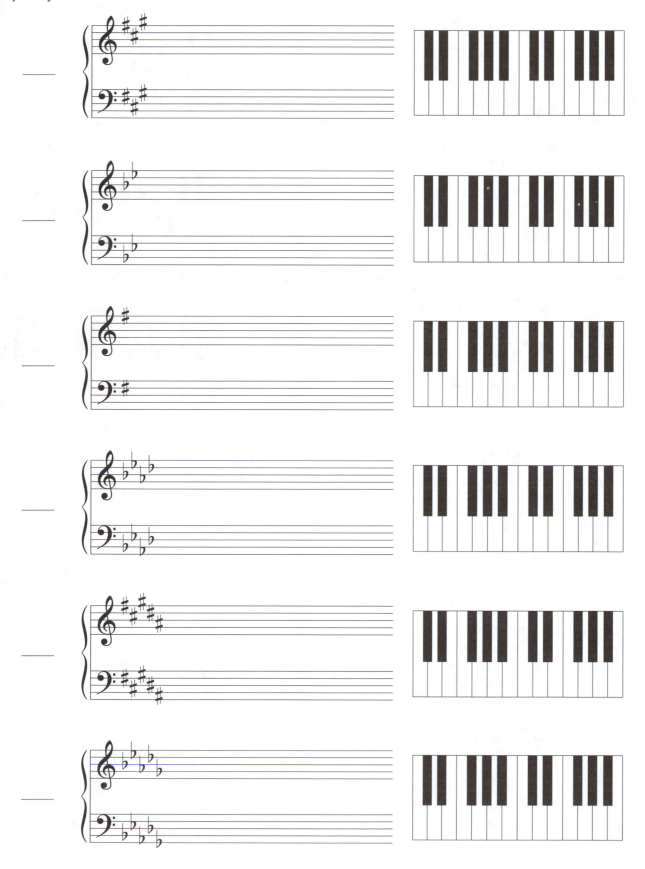

Major Key Name

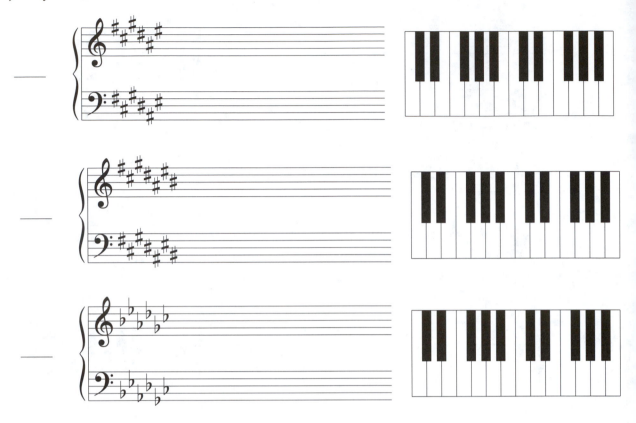

PRACTICE

Writing the Circle of Fifths

Complete the circle of fifths for major keys.

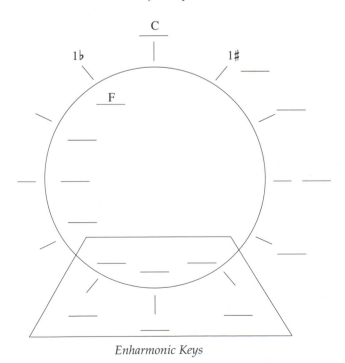

Enharmonic Keys

MUSICAL APPLICATION

Reading and Singing Melodies

1. Outline the contour of each melody.

2. Write the scale-degree number or the melodic syllable for each note in these exercises. Write in a moderate tempo (M.M.) at the beginning of each exercise—use a metronome to set the tempo. Find the beginning notes on a keyboard before singing a melody.

3. Put in dynamic markings, and sing each exercise again.

MUSICAL APPLICATION

Listening to Music in Major Keys

Study each excerpt. What major scale is associated with each key signature? The last note in each example is the *keynote,* or tonic, and should reinforce your identification of key by key signature. Play and sing the scale on which each work is based before you listen to the excerpt.

A MIGHTY FORTRESS IS OUR GOD (R-34)
from Cantata No. 80

Johann Sebastian Bach
(Germany, 1685–1750)

Key _____

Ein fe - ste Burg ist un - ser Gott, ein gu - te Wehr und _ Waf   -   ten;
Er hilft uns frei _ aus al - ler Not, die uns jetzt hat be - trof - fen.

CONCERTO GROSSO OP. 6, NO. 1

George Frideric Handel
(Germany, 1685–1759)

Key _____

THIRD MOVEMENT (R-35)
from Sonata No. 35

Franz Joseph Haydn
(Austria, 1732–1809)

Key _____

IMPROMPTU OP. 142, NO. 2, D. 935 (R-36)

Franz Schubert
(Austria, 1797–1828)

Key _____

(continued)

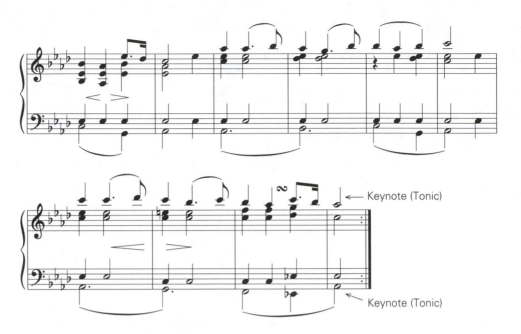

Keynote (Tonic)

Keynote (Tonic)

MUSICAL APPLICATION

Playing Melodies in Major Keys on a Keyboard

Many melodies have five or fewer consecutive pitches and can be played with the right hand on a keyboard without adjustment of hand position. Begin by playing the first five notes of the scale that is related to the piece. Then play the pitches and the correct rhythm, which combine to create the musical element we call melody.

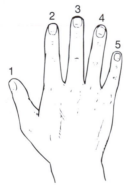

FIVE-FINGER PATTERN IN THE F MAJOR SCALE

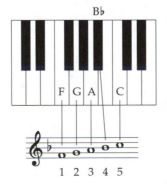

FOLK DANCE

France

FIVE-FINGER PATTERN IN THE G MAJOR SCALE

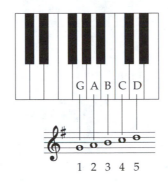

JINGLE BELLS
(excerpt)

U.S.A.

Jin - gle bells, Jin - gle bells, Jin - gle all the way.

O what fun it is to ride in a one horse o - pen sleigh, __ one horse o - pen sleigh,

LIGHTLY ROW

Germany

CHORALE
from *The St. Matthew Passion*

Johann Sebastian Bach
(Germany, 1685–1750)

FIVE-FINGER PATTERN IN THE C MAJOR SCALE

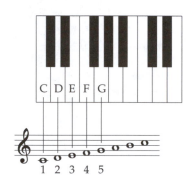

PEASE PORRIDGE HOT

Traditional

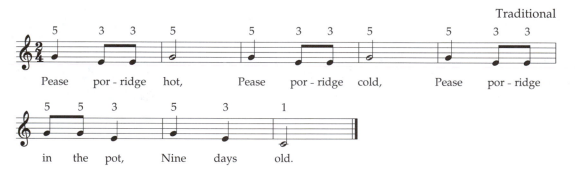

Pease por-ridge hot, Pease por-ridge cold, Pease por-ridge

in the pot, Nine days old.

2. Some like it hot,
   Some like it cold,
   Some like it in the pot,
   Nine days old.

DINAH

U.S.A.

No one in the house but Di - nah, Di - nah, No one in the house but me I know.

No one in the house but Di - nah, Di - nah, Strum-min' on the old ban - jo.

"Aura Lee" uses the five-finger pattern found in C major, although the song is actually in F major. (See the last note of the song and the key signature.)

AURA LEE

Fa in F major

U.S.A.

As the black-bird in the spring, 'Neath the wil-low tree, _____

Sat and piped, I heard him sing, Sing-ing Au-ra Lee.   F Major

TRANSPOSITION

Transposition is the rewriting of a musical score in a new key. Sometimes, a musical work is notated in a key that is too high or too low for the voices that will perform it, or is in a key that is difficult to play on a particular instrument. We can move the notes to a more accommodating key quite easily.

"We Shall Overcome" is in C major. If the singers find it pitched too high for their vocal ranges, we can move it down a step to the key of B-flat major, or down two steps to the key of A-flat major, and so on. The song will then have a lower pitch range.

To transpose a song, follow these steps:

1. Write out the scale of the key in which the song is presently notated.
2. Write the scale-degree numbers under the notes in the song.
3. Write out the scale of the desired key and its scale-degree numbers.
4. Determine the new notes in the transposed song by matching numbers.

EXAMPLE

The key of the song is presently C major.

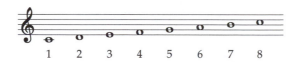

The song will be transposed to B-flat major.

WE SHALL OVERCOME

Civil Rights Song

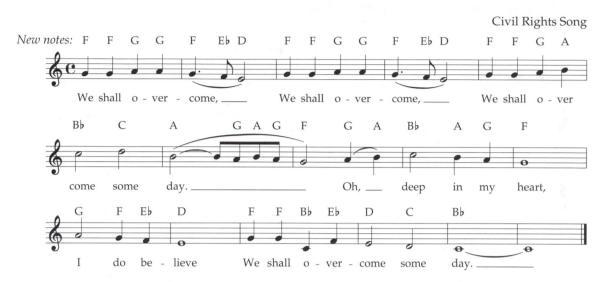

Sing the first line of "We Shall Overcome" in the original key, C major, then in the transposed version in B-flat major, shown below. Observe that each note is one whole step lower in the transposed version.

WE SHALL OVERCOME

(transposed to B♭ major)

Civil Rights Song

Transposing by Interval

As you become more proficient at transposition, you will be able to transpose by interval, or distance between notes. For example, transposing from E-flat major up to G major moves each note in the transposed version up two whole steps. Transposing down from E-flat major to C major moves each note in the transposed version down one and one-half steps.

MUSICAL APPLICATION

Transposing Songs and Melodic Phrases

Transpose "Amazing Grace" from G major to F major, following the scheme used to transpose "We Shall Overcome" or the method described under Transposing by Interval.

AMAZING GRACE

John Newton
(England, 1725–1807)

American Folk Hymn

1. Write the G major scale and its scale-degree numbers here.

2. Write the F major scale and its scale-degree numbers here.

3. Notate "Amazing Grace" in F major.

Transpose "In the Bleak Midwinter" from F major down to E-flat major. What is the distance between F and E-flat (descending)? Move each note in the song down that distance.

IN THE BLEAK MIDWINTER

Christina Rossetti
(England, 1830–1894)

Gustav Holst
(England, 1874–1934)

Transpose "The Wabash Cannon Ball" from G major to A-flat major.

THE WABASH CANNON BALL

U.S.A.

Transpose "America" from F major to D-flat major.

AMERICA
(excerpt)

Henry Carey   Samuel Smith

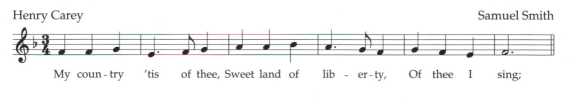

My coun-try 'tis of thee, Sweet land of lib-er-ty, Of thee I sing;

REVIEW OF TERMS

Define each term. Where appropriate, draw, notate, or present in a musical context to demonstrate your understanding.

1. scale
2. chromatic scale
3. half step
4. whole step
5. major scale
6. pitch classes
7. diatonic
8. C major scale
9. key
10. key of C major
11. tonic
12. melodic syllable names
13. tonic *sol-fa*
14. movable *do*
15. scale-degree names
16. key signature
17. G major scale
18. F major scale
19. circle of fifths
20. enharmonic keys
21. transposition

WORKSHEET
Chapter 4 Review

1. Write the name of the major key that is associated with each key signature.

2. How many pitches are included in an octave? _____

3. If all the pitches in an octave are played successively from lowest to highest, or highest to lowest, what scale is heard? _____

4. Describe a diatonic scale.

5. What are the principal features of a major scale?

6. The first pitch in a major scale is the tonic. What are the other scale-degree names? _____, _____, _____, _____, _____,

_____.

7. Are black keys on the keyboard always needed to create half steps between steps 3 and 4 of a major scale? Explain.

8. In the circle of fifths, the sharp keys are shown on the (right   left) of the circle; the flat keys are shown on the (right   left) of the circle. The distance between the names of the keys in either direction is _____.

9. From which of its pitches does a major scale derive its name? _____

10. Complete the right side of this chart.

If the	The major key is
a. leading tone is D-sharp	**a.**
b. mediant is E	**b.**
c. supertonic is A	**c.**
d. subdominant is B-flat	**d.**
e. dominant is C-sharp	**e.**
f. submediant is A-flat	**f.**
g. leading tone is C	**g.**
h. supertonic is A-flat	**h.**
i. dominant is F-sharp	**i.**
j. submediant is G	**j.**
k. mediant is D	**k.**
l. subdominant is G-flat	**l.**

11. Write an H beside each half step; write a W beside each whole step.

a. A–B _____   **f.** G♯–F𝄪 _____

b. F–E♭ _____   **g.** C♭–D♭♭ _____

c. G♭–F _____   **h.** E–F♯ _____

d. C♯–D♯ _____   **i.** B♭–C _____

e. A♯–B _____   **j.** D♭–C♭ _____

CHAPTER PROJECTS

1. Find the score for a favorite carol, hymn, or folk song in a major key. Transpose it up a half step, then down two whole steps. Follow the procedures you used in the section on transposition, pp. 103–107. Play it on a keyboard in the three keys.

2. Complete each four-bar phrase. End the first one on the tonic note, *do*. End the second phrase on the fifth, or *sol*, of the key's scale. Which one sounds complete?

3. What major key do you associate with each of these examples?
   a. "The Star-Spangled Banner," p. 42
   b. "Worried Man," p. 63
   c. "She'll Be Comin' 'Round the Mountain," p. 53
   d. "The Viennese Musical Clock," by Zoltán Kodály, p. 70
   e. "Farandole," from *L'Arlésienne* Suite No. 2, by Georges Bizet, p. 50

CHAPTER **5**

Minor Scales and Keys

MINOR SCALES

Minor, the Latin word for "smaller," refers to the difference between the major and minor scales. The third degree is one half step lower in the minor scale than in the major, making the distance between the second and third degrees smaller than in the major, or "larger," scale. Compare the C major and the C minor scales on the staff. Then locate the notes of each scale on a keyboard.

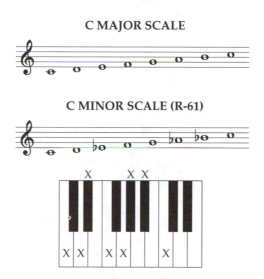

C MAJOR SCALE

C MINOR SCALE (R-61)

Another difference between major and minor scales is that the minor scale has three forms: natural, harmonic, and melodic. Each form of the minor scale has its own pattern of half steps and whole steps that is appropriate in musical settings for writing melodies or accompanying melodies with harmony.

Minor scales beginning on the same tonic, regardless of form, share the same key signature. Alterations of the natural minor that occur in the harmonic and melodic minor forms appear as accidentals in the scales. Therefore, we will begin our study of the minor scale with the natural form.

The Natural Minor Scale

Like the major scale, the *natural minor scale* is made up of five whole steps and two half steps, but the pattern is different. Compare the arrangements of half steps and whole steps in these scales (⌵ = half step):

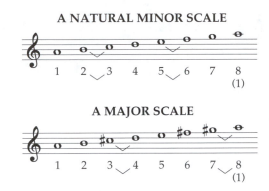

The A natural minor scale, like the C major scale, is played on white keys only. Accidentals are needed for the other natural minor scales.

Names of Scale Degrees in Natural Minor   In the natural minor scale, the seventh degree is one whole step from the tonic and is called the *subtonic.* In minor keys, the term *leading tone* is used when, as in major, the seventh degree is one half step from the tonic.

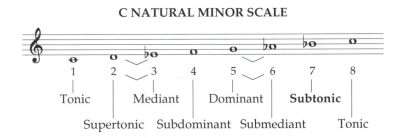

Sight-Reading in Minor Keys

Reading is facilitated in minor keys, as in major keys, by identifying scale degrees by letter names, numbers, and melodic syllables. The tonic in a minor key is named *la,* and the scale is named accordingly for melodic reading.

MUSICAL APPLICATION

Singing a Song in C Minor

Use one of the sight-reading systems to assist you in learning this song. Outline the contour. Write in melodic syllables, or use numbers.

THE WRAGGLE TAGGLE GYPSIES

Old English

There were three_ gyp-sies a-come to my door, And down-stairs ran this a-la-dy, O!   The

one   sang high, And an-oth-er sang low, And the oth-er sang bon-ny, bon-ny Bis-cay. O!

MINOR KEY SIGNATURES

The Circle of Fifths, Minor Keys

You have studied the natural form of the A and C minor keys. There are thirteen other minor keys, each with its own key signature. Once you have learned these key signatures, you can apply them to all three forms of the minor scale. (The other two forms are covered later in this chapter following practice with the key signatures and writing the natural minor scales.)

As it is for the major keys, the *circle of fifths* is a helpful visual aid in learning the minor key signatures.

The key of A minor, which has neither sharps nor flats, is at the top of the circle. Sharp keys, which use from one to seven sharps in their signatures, are shown moving clockwise from A minor. Flat keys, which use from one to seven flats, are shown moving counterclockwise from A. *Enharmonic keys,* which have different signatures but sound alike, are shown overlapping at the bottom of the circle.

As in the circle of fifths for major keys, the key names moving in either direction are seven half steps, or a perfect fifth, apart. Moving seven half steps up the keyboard from A to locate the minor key with one sharp, we arrive at E. Moving seven half steps from E on the keyboard, we arrive at B, the name of the minor key with two sharps. To locate the key names for flat minor keys, we move seven half steps down the keyboard from A and arrive at D, the minor key with one flat. From D, we move down another perfect fifth and arrive at G, the name of the minor key with two flats.

THE CIRCLE OF FIFTHS, MINOR KEYS

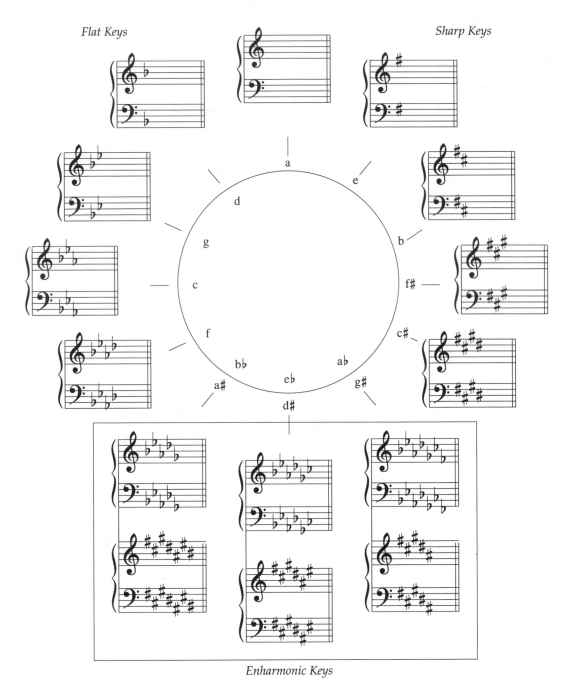

Flat Keys   *Sharp Keys*

Enharmonic Keys

Minor Scales with Sharps

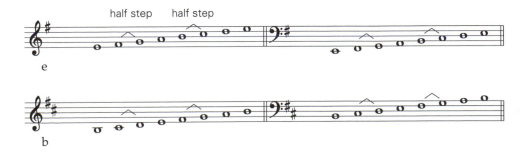

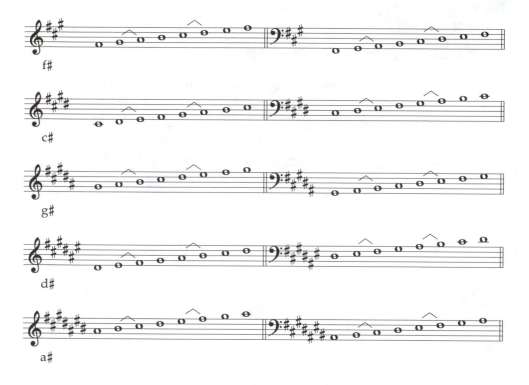

Minor Scales with Flats

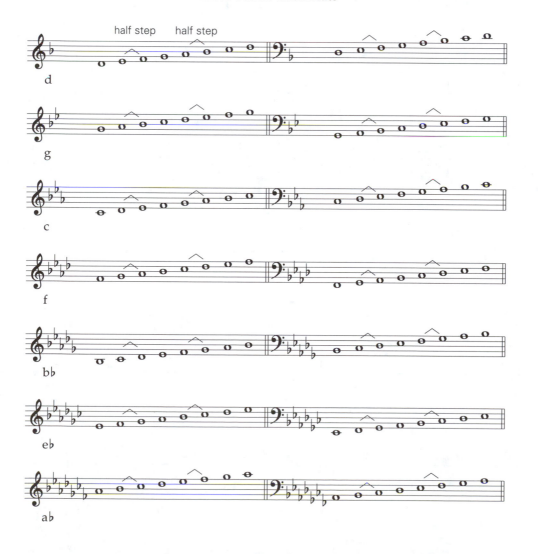

PRACTICE

Placing Key Signatures on the Staff

On the blank staves, copy each key signature, observing carefully the placement of the flats and sharps around or between lines. Write the letter name of the minor key associated with each signature in the blank between the staves.

PRACTICE

Writing the Circle of Fifths

Complete the circle of fifths for minor keys.

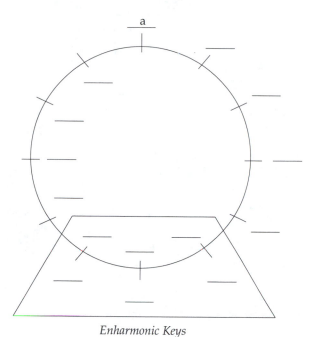

Enharmonic Keys

PRACTICE

Writing the Minor Key Signatures and Scales

Write the key signature and the natural minor scale associated with each minor key name. Write letter names, scale-degree numbers, and melodic syllables under each note written after the bass clef. The key names are in the order found on the circle of fifths, beginning with sharp keys. Then mark scale notes on the keyboard with X's.

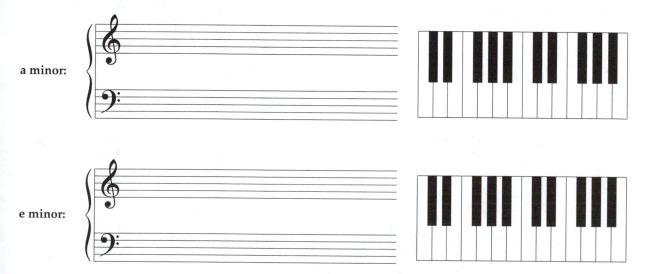

a minor:

e minor:

b minor:

f# minor:

c# minor:

g# minor:

d# minor:

a# minor:

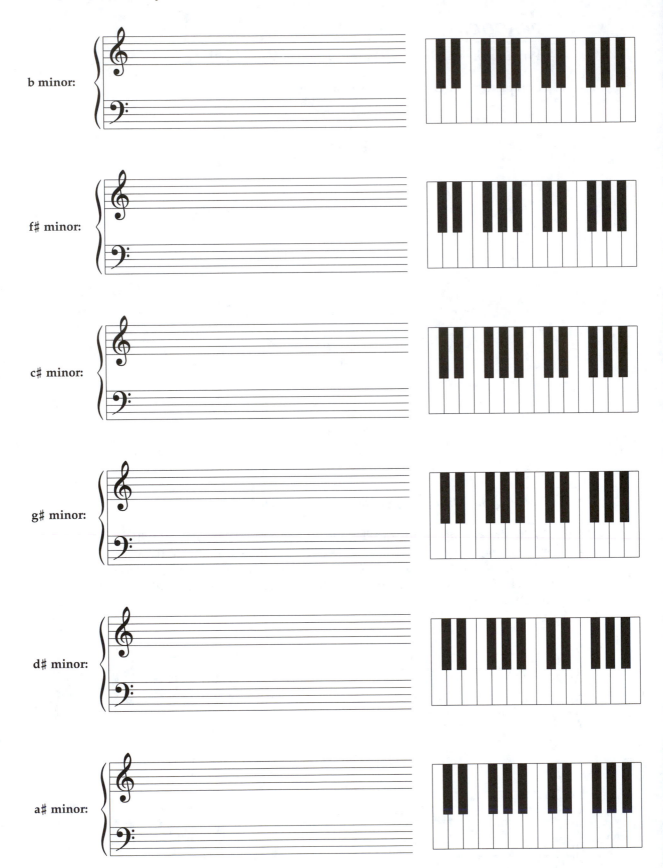

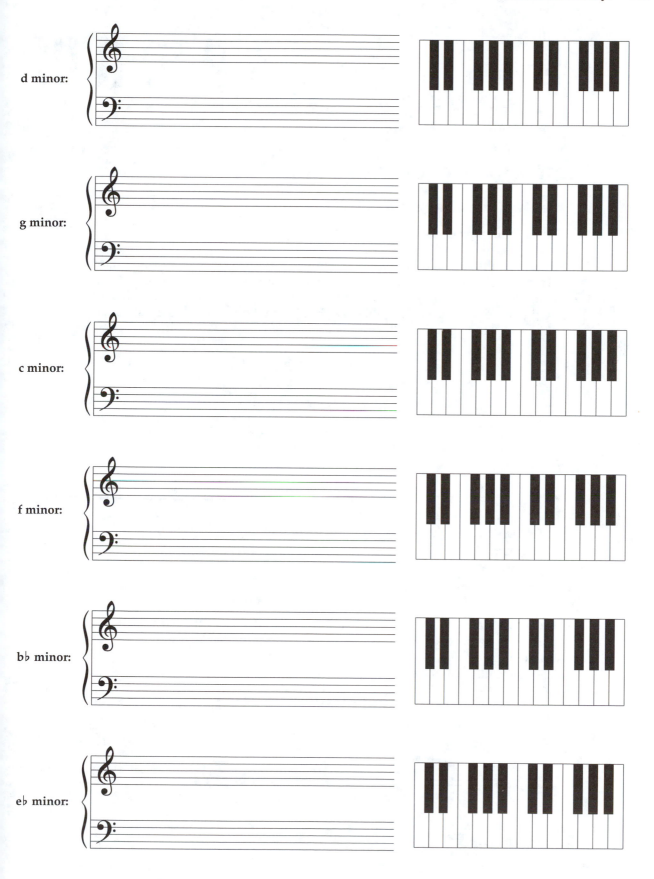

d minor:

g minor:

c minor:

f minor:

b♭ minor:

e♭ minor:

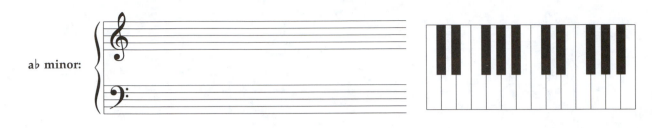

ab minor:

OTHER FORMS OF THE MINOR SCALE

The Harmonic Minor Scale

The *harmonic minor scale* is created when the seventh degree of the natural minor scale is raised one half step. The seventh degree is then labeled the *leading tone*, rather than the subtonic, because of its strong pull toward the tonic. The distance between the sixth and seventh scale degrees is three half steps. Remember that the raised seventh degree is indicated by an accidental, since it is not found in the key signature. The melodic syllable associated with the seventh degree is changed from *sol* to *si* to reflect the half-step alteration.

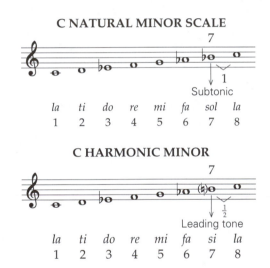

Use of the Harmonic Minor

The raised seventh degree of the harmonic minor is used by composers primarily in harmonic settings, particularly at the close of a section or piece. This example shows the increased drive toward closure that the raised seventh tone creates.

GIB DICH ZUFRIEDEN UND SEI STILLE

Johann Sebastian Bach
(Germany, 1685–1750)

PRACTICE

Spelling Harmonic Minor Scales

Spell the harmonic minor scale associated with each minor key named below. Remember to raise the seventh degree of the natural minor scale one half step. The sharps and flats are written *after* the letter names.

Minor Key Name

C   ____ ____ ____ ____ ____ ____ ____

F♯   ____ ____ ____ ____ ____ ____ ____

A   ____ ____ ____ ____ ____ ____ ____

C♯   ____ ____ ____ ____ ____ ____ ____

G   ____ ____ ____ ____ ____ ____ ____

B♭   ____ ____ ____ ____ ____ ____ ____

D   ____ ____ ____ ____ ____ ____ ____

F   ____ ____ ____ ____ ____ ____ ____

G♯   ____ ____ ____ ____ ____ ____ ____

B   ____ ____ ____ ____ ____ ____ ____

D♯   ____ ____ ____ ____ ____ ____ ____

E♭   ____ ____ ____ ____ ____ ____ ____

A♯   ____ ____ ____ ____ ____ ____ ____

E   ____ ____ ____ ____ ____ ____ ____

A♭   ____ ____ ____ ____ ____ ____ ____

The Melodic Minor Scale

The *melodic minor scale* is the only scale with different ascending and descending patterns. It is based on the common practice of composers to raise the sixth degree of the ascending scale in melodic writing to avoid the step-and-one-half distance between scale degrees 6 and 7 that occurs when the leading tone, or seventh degree, is raised. The descending pattern is the natural-scale pattern. Note that the melodic syllables are adapted to the altered tones.

G HARMONIC MINOR (R-62)

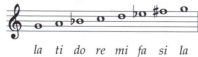

la   ti   do   re   mi   fa   si   la

G MELODIC MINOR (R-63)

la   ti   do   re   mi   fi*   si   la   la   sol   fa   mi   re   do   ti   la

*Fa raised one half step is fi.

Study these examples of the use of the melodic minor scale in melody.

**DESCENDING AND ASCENDING FORMS
OF THE G MELODIC MINOR SCALE**

CONCERTO GROSSO IN G MINOR, OP. 3/2

Antonio Vivaldi
(Italy, 1678–1741)

ASCENDING FORM OF THE C MELODIC MINOR SCALE

FIRST MOVEMENT
from Piano Concerto No. 3

Ludwig van Beethoven
(Germany, 1770–1827)

PRACTICE

Writing Melodic Minor Scales

Write the key name associated with each key signature. Then write the appropriate melodic minor scale, in both ascending and descending forms.

Key Name   **Ascending Scale**   **Descending Scale**

Key Name	Ascending Scale	Descending Scale

Key Name   **Ascending Scale**   **Descending Scale**

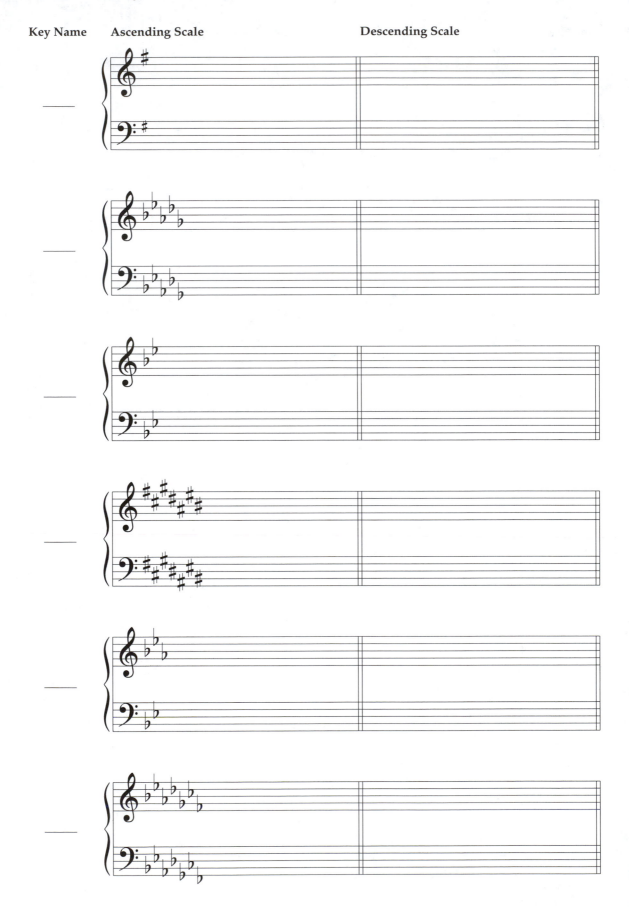

good old work-er and a good old pal, Fif-teen miles on the E - rie Ca - nal. We've

hauled some barg - es in our day, Filled with lum - ber, coal and hay, And

we know ev - ery inch of the way From Al - ba- ny ___ to ___ Buf - fa - lo. ___

Chorus

Low bridge, ev - ery-bod - y down, Low bridge, 'cause we're

com - ing to a town; And you'll al - ways know your neigh - bor, You'll

al - ways know your pal, If you've ev - er nav - i-gat - ed on the E - rie Ca - nal.

Parallel Keys

A minor key and a major key that share the same tonic note but have different key signatures are called *parallel keys.* D major and D minor both have tonic D's, but they have different signatures.

PRACTICE

Study the parallel key signatures for each pair of tonic notes.

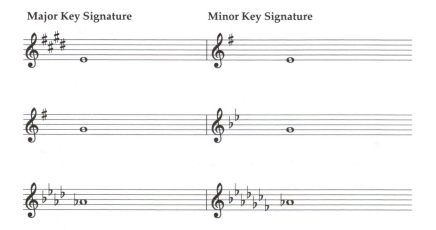

MUSICAL APPLICATION

Singing in Minor Keys

In the space provided, write the name of the minor key that is associated with each song. Above the notes, write melodic syllables with *la* as the tonic note. Remember that the seventh scale degree in harmonic minor is called *si*. Sing the songs with your classmates.

1. _____ _____
    Key   Type of minor scale

JOHNNY HAS GONE FOR A SOLDIER

U.S.A.

Sad I sit on But-ter-nut Hill. Who could blame me cry my fill? And ev-'ry tear would turn a mill, John-ny has gone for a sol - dier.

2. _____ _____
    Key   Type of minor scale

THE FROG AND THE MOUSE

England

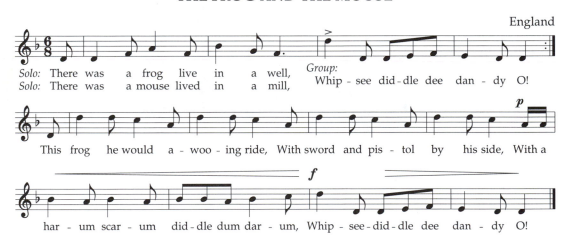

Solo: There was a frog live in a well,
Solo: There was a mouse lived in a mill, *Group:* Whip - see did - dle dee dan - dy O!

This frog he would a - woo - ing ride, With sword and pis - tol by his side, With a

har - um scar - um did - dle dum dar - um, Whip - see - did - dle dee dan - dy O!

3. _____ _____
    Key   Type of minor scale

ÜSKÜDAR

Turkish Folk Song

Üs - kü-dar' a gi - der __ i ken al - li-da bir yağ mur,
uhs - kuh-dahr ah gih - dehr ih kehn ahl - lih-dah bihr yahj muhr

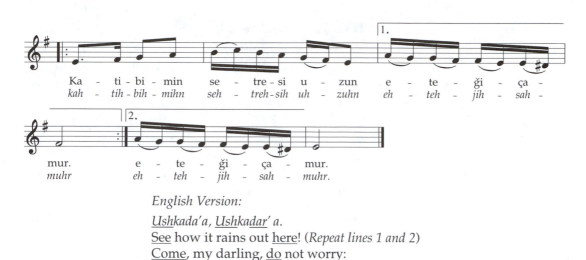

Ka - ti - bi - min se - tre - si u - zun e - te - ği - ça -
kah - tih - bih - mihn seh - treh - sih uh - zuhn eh - teh - jih - sah -

mur.   e - te - ği - ça - mur.
muhr.   eh - teh - jih - sah - muhr.

English Version:

Ushkada'a, Ushkadar' a.
See how it rains out here! (*Repeat lines 1 and 2*)
Come, my darling, do not worry:
Love will keep us warm! (*Repeat lines 3 and 4*)

MUSICAL APPLICATION

Listening to Music in Minor Keys

The following excerpts are main themes from significant instrumental compositions. Although most convey somber, sad, or plaintive moods, one, Hungarian Dance No. 5, is a lively dance; another, "The Moldau," is a celebration of a beautiful river as it meanders through the Bohemian countryside. Remember that non-Western cultures do not always associate minor keys with either slow tempi or serious affects.

THIRD MOVEMENT (R-37)
from Piano Sonata, Op. 26

Ludwig van Beethoven
(Germany, 1770–1827)

Maestoso andante

SECOND MOVEMENT (R-38)
from Symphony No. 4 in A Major (*Italian*)

Felix Mendelssohn
(Germany, 1809–1847)

After introduction:

THE MOLDAU (R-39)
from *Ma Vlast* (My Country)
(first theme)

Bedřich Smetana
(Bohemia, 1824–1884)

LITTLE FUGUE IN G MINOR (R-40)

Johann Sebastian Bach
(Germany, 1685–1750)

HUNGARIAN DANCE No. 5 (R-41)

Johannes Brahms
(Germany, 1833–1897)

SECOND MOVEMENT (R-42)
from Symphony in D Minor
(first theme)

César Franck
(France, 1822–1890)

MUSICAL APPLICATION

Playing Melodies in Minor Keys on a Keyboard

Continue your exploration of the keyboard by playing the first five notes of the scale for each piece. Then play the pitches and the correct rhythm, which combine to create the musical element we call melody.

FIVE-FINGER PATTERN IN THE D MINOR SCALE

TWO SLAVIC MELODIES

FIVE-FINGER PATTERN IN THE E MINOR SCALE

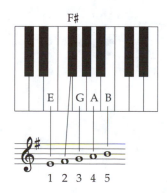

SKATER'S WALTZ

Traditional

YA HA E

With spirit in moderate time (M.M. ♩ = 144)

American Indian

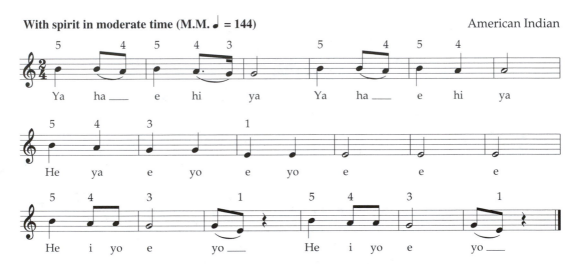

Ya ha ___ e   hi   ya   Ya ha ___ e   hi   ya

He ya   e   yo   e   yo   e   e   e

He i yo   e   yo ___   He i yo   e   yo ___

Pronunciation Guide:

e is pronounced like long *a*
he is pronounced like *hey*
i is like the *i* in *him*

FINALE
from Symphony No. 4
(excerpt)

Peter I. Tchaikovsky
(Russia, 1840—1893

PRACTICE

Transposing Music in Minor Keys

To transpose music from one minor key to another, you should follow the same rules that apply to major keys. (See Chapter 4.) Here are two assignments for you to complete.

1. Transpose the theme of the second movement of Mendelssohn's Symphony No. 4, p. 129, from D minor to C minor.

2. Transpose "Johnny Has Gone for a Soldier," p. 128, from G minor to A minor.

REVIEW OF TERMS

Define each term. Where appropriate, draw, notate, or present in a musical context to demonstrate your understanding.

1. minor
2. major
3. C minor scale
4. natural minor scale
5. A natural minor scale
6. scale degrees (in minor)
7. melodic syllables (in minor)
8. circle of fifths (minor keys)
9. harmonic minor scale
10. C harmonic minor scale
11. melodic minor scale
12. G harmonic minor scale
13. relative keys
14. parallel keys

WORKSHEET
Chapter 5 Review

1. *Minor* is the Latin word meaning _____.

2. *Major* is the Latin word meaning _____.

3. How does your definition in question 1 relate to the minor scale?

_____

4. How do major and minor scales differ? _____

_____

5. How many whole steps and half steps are in the natural minor scale?

_____ whole steps; _____ half steps

6. Which scale degree in natural minor is different from the major-scale degrees?

_____ What is its name in natural minor? _____

7. Melodic syllables in major are *do re mi fa sol la ti do.* What is one way they can

be arranged in minor? _____

8. On the circle of fifths that illustrates minor keys, which key is at the top of the

circle, representing no flats and no sharps? _____ What is its relative major key, also

representing no flats and no sharps? _____

9. What is the name of the minor key associated with these numbers of sharps and
flats?

6 sharps _____	7 flats _____
3 flats _____	1 sharp _____
1 flat _____	0 flats _____
4 sharps _____	4 flats _____
0 sharps _____	7 sharps _____
2 sharps _____	5 flats _____
2 flats _____	6 flats _____
5 sharps _____	3 sharps _____

10. Write key signatures for these parallel keys:

11. Write the name of the relative minor key of each major key.

G major _____   B-flat major _____

F-sharp major _____   E major _____

D-flat major _____   C-sharp major _____

C major _____   F major _____

A major _____   A-flat major _____

E-flat major _____   B major _____

12. Write the names of the three pairs of enharmonic minor key signatures on the circle of fifths.

_____ and _____

_____ and _____

_____ and _____

13. Change this natural minor scale to harmonic minor.

G A B♭ C D E♭ F G _____

14. Change this natural minor scale to melodic minor.

F♯ G♯ A B C♯ D E F♯ _____   _____

                           (ascending)   (descending)

15. Go back to questions 13 and 14. Write the melodic syllables and scale-degree numbers under the notes.

16. Identify each melody your instructor plays as either major (M) or minor (m).

    a. _____

    b. _____

    c. _____

    d. _____

    e. _____

17. Write the harmonic minor scale and the relative major scale associated with each natural minor scale.

Natural Minor:

Harmonic Minor:

Relative Major:

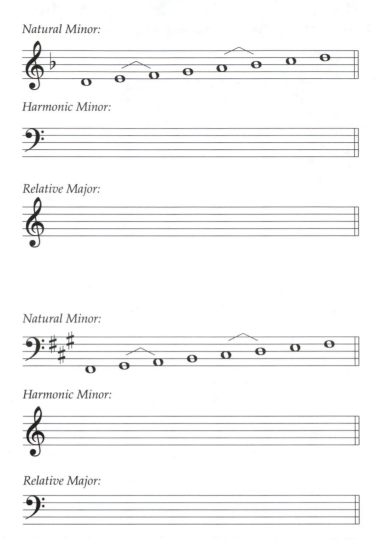

Natural Minor:

Harmonic Minor:

Relative Major:

Natural Minor:

Harmonic Minor:

Relative Major:

CHAPTER PROJECTS

1. Listen to these pieces. Are they in major or minor keys?
   a. Grand March (*Aida*), by Giuseppe Verdi (R-5)
   b. March (*Love for Three Oranges*), by Sergei Prokofiev (R-12)
   c. Waltz, Op. 69, No. 2, by Frédéric Chopin (R-22)
   d. "Oranges and Lemons," English folk song (R-10)

2. Rewrite "The Moldau" theme, p. 130, in its parallel major key. Listen as your instructor plays both the minor and the major versions.

3. Locate a book of hymns, carols, or folk tunes. Determine whether each work is major or minor by looking at the key signature, checking the final note (which almost always is the tonic and therefore the key name), and checking for raised sixth and seventh degrees, which indicate melodic or harmonic minor keys. Remember that accidentals for melodic and harmonic minor are not in the key signatures but appear beside the notes they affect.

Rhythm III: Advanced Concepts

In this chapter, you will be introduced to more-advanced rhythm concepts, including compound meters, syncopation, and irregular rhythmic organization. Your ability to read rhythm, pitch, and expressive markings simultaneously will be heightened by challenging song and listening selections and practice exercises.

COMPOUND METER

The rhythms of *compound meter* are those most often associated with the English language. They are found in dance music, pop music, folk music of British and Latin origins, and art music from the Baroque to the contemporary period.

In the simple meters we have studied, the beat is divided into two equal parts. *In compound meter, the beat is divided into three equal parts.*

The following examples illustrate the difference between a simple and a compound meter, each using six eighth notes.

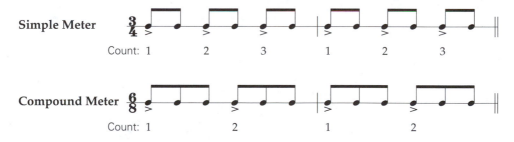

In the preceding examples, observe that in the simple meter, each beat is divided into two parts, with three groups of two notes in each measure. In the compound meter, there is the same number of eighth notes, but there are *two groups of three notes* in each measure. Tap the examples while stepping the accents with your foot.

In compound meter signatures, the top number is divisible by three and the bottom number represents the beat division (4, 8, or 16). Interpret compound meter signatures this way:

6
8   Divide by 3 to determine the number of pulses per measure (2).
Multiply by 3 (♪ + ♪ + ♪) to determine the note equal to one beat (♩.).

Tap this example:

Count: 1   2   1   2

9
16   Divide by 3 to determine the number of beats per measure (3).
Multiply by 3 (♪ + ♪ + ♪) to determine the note equal to one beat (♪.).

Tap this example:

Count: 1   2   3   1   2   3

6
4   Divide by 3 (two beats per measure).
Multiply by 3. (♩. = one beat).

Tap this example:

Count: 1   2   1   2

When we relate simple and compound meters to language, we can feel the differences readily.

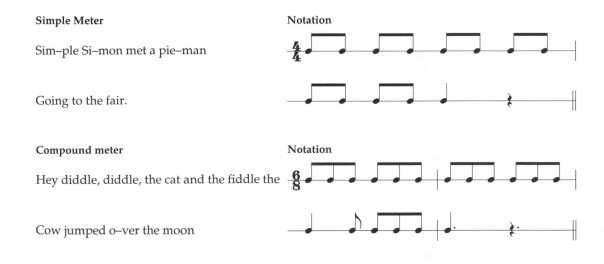

Simple Meter   **Notation**

Sim–ple Si–mon met a pie–man

Going to the fair.

Compound meter   **Notation**

Hey diddle, diddle, the cat and the fiddle the

Cow jumped o–ver the moon

PRACTICE

Tapping Beat Units, Divisions, and Subdivisions in Compound Meter

In compound meter, the beat unit is a dotted note. Here is a chart showing beat units in compound meter with their divisions and subdivisions. Learn these by tapping the beats with your left hand and the divisions and subdivisions with your right hand. Practice each exercise in both slow and fast tempi.

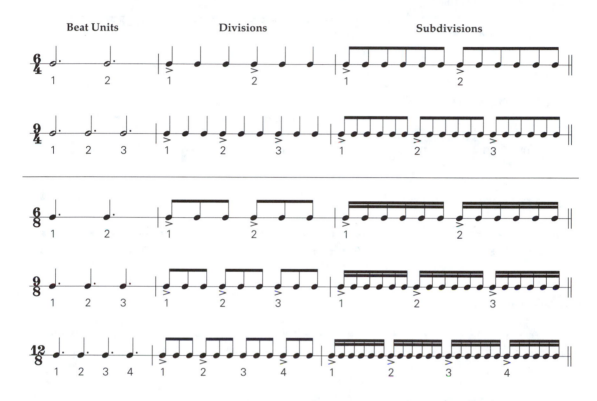

Study the following compound meter signatures and their translation into beats per measure and beat units, shown in parentheses. Observe that the beat-division numbers (6, 9, and 12) always result in duple, triple, and quadruple meter and that the division of the beats into quarter, eighth, and sixteenth notes creates dotted beat units (dotted half notes, dotted quarter notes, and dotted eighth notes).

COMPOUND METER SIGNATURES

	Duple	Triple	Quadruple
	$\frac{6}{16}$ (2 ♪.)	$\frac{9}{16}$ (3 ♪.)	$\frac{12}{16}$ (4 ♪.)
Used most often	$\frac{6}{8}$ (2 ♩.)	$\frac{9}{8}$ (3 ♩.)	$\frac{12}{8}$ (4 ♩.)
	$\frac{6}{4}$ (2 ♩.)	$\frac{9}{4}$ (3 ♩.)	$\frac{12}{4}$ (4 ♩.)

PRACTICE

Counting in Compound Meters

Tap or clap these patterns in compound meters with your instructor's assistance. Keep the beat in 2, 3, or 4 with your foot. Count aloud with the numbers and syllables.

COMPOUND DUPLE METER

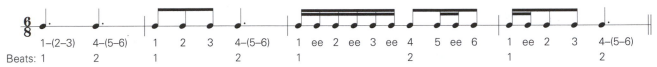

| 1–(2–3) | 4–(5–6) | 1 | 2 | 3 | 4–(5–6) | 1 | ee | 2 | ee | 3 | ee | 4 | 5 | ee | 6 | 1 | ee | 2 | 3 | 4–(5–6) |
Beats: 1   2   1   2   1   2   1   2

COMPOUND TRIPLE METER

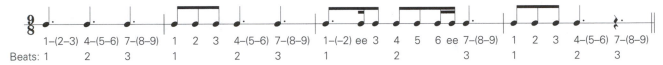

| 1–(2–3) | 4–(5–6) | 7–(8–9) | 1 | 2 | 3 | 4–(5–6) | 7–(8–9) | 1–(–2) ee 3 | 4 | 5 | 6 ee 7–(8–9) | 1 | 2 | 3 | 4–(5–6) | 7–(8–9) |
Beats: 1   2   3   1   2   3   1   2   3   1   2   3

COMPOUND QUADRUPLE METER

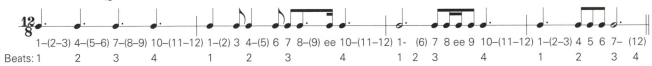

| 1–(2–3) 4–(5–6) 7–(8–9) 10–(11–12) | 1–(2) 3 4–(5) 6 7 8–(9) ee 10–(11–12) | 1– (6) 7 8 ee 9 10–(11–12) | 1–(2–3) 4 5 6 7– (12) |
Beats: 1   2   3   4   1   2   3   4   1 2 3   4   1   2   3 4

COMPOUND DUPLE METER

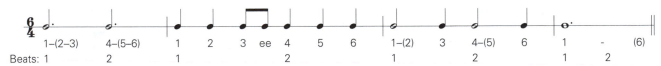

| 1–(2–3) | 4–(5–6) | 1 | 2 | 3 ee 4 | 5 | 6 | 1–(2) | 3 | 4–(5) | 6 | 1 | - | (6) |
Beats: 1   2   1   2   1   2   1   2

COMPOUND TRIPLE METER

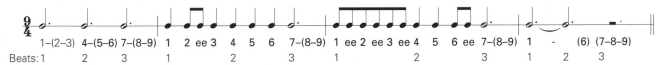

| 1–(2–3) | 4–(5–6) | 7–(8–9) | 1 | 2 ee 3 | 4 | 5 | 6 | 7–(8–9) | 1 ee 2 ee 3 ee 4 | 5 | 6 ee 7–(8–9) | 1 | - | (6) (7–8–9) |
Beats: 1   2   3   1   2   3   1   2   3   1   2   3

Tap and count the following exercises with your classmates. Group 1 should perform the top line and group 2 the bottom line. Then exchange assignments. If percussion instruments are available, use two different timbres (for example, drums and woodblocks). In the space to the left of each example, write S (simple) or C (compound) to identify the meter.

MUSICAL APPLICATION

Singing in Compound Meters

Listen to your instructor's presentation of each song or excerpt in compound meter. Which have two groups of three beats? Three groups of three beats? Count the rhythms of each song; then sing it.

PAT WORKS ON THE RAILWAY
(*excerpt*)

Irish American Work Song

In eigh - teen hun-dred and for - ty one I put me cor-du-roy brit - ches on. I

put me cor-du-roy brit - ches on to work up on the rail - way.

GREENSLEEVES

England (ca. 1580)

A - las my love _ you do me wrong _ to cast me off _ dis-court-eous-ly: And

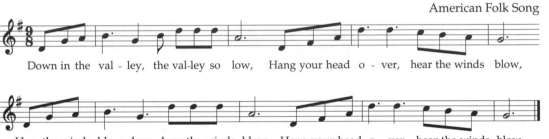

I have loved you for so long. Delighting in your company.

Chorus

Green-sleeves was all my joy. Green-sleeves was my delight.

Green-sleeves was my heart of gold And who but my lady Green-sleeves.

DOWN IN THE VALLEY

American Folk Song

Down in the valley, the valley so low, Hang your head over, hear the winds blow,

Hear the winds blow, dear, hear the winds blow, Hang your head over, hear the winds blow.

MUSICAL APPLICATION

Listening to Music in Compound Meters

Listen to these excerpts in compound meters. Notice that the first example is counted in 6, with each beat division receiving a conducting gesture, a consistent practice in slow tempi. The other examples illustrate the use of the beat-unit pulse.

1. Count in 6: Slow compound duple meter.

FIRST MOVEMENT
from Symphony No. 1 in C Minor, Op. 68

Johnannes Brahms
(Germany, 1833–1897)

2. Count in 2: Compound duple meter.

THIRD MOVEMENT (R-43)
from Piano Concerto No. 2 in B flat Major, Op. 19
(theme)

3. Count in 3: Compound triple meter.

PRELUDE XX IN A MINOR (R-44)
from *The Well-Tempered Clavier,* Book I

4. Count in 4: Compound quadruple meter.

SECOND MOVMENT
from Symphony No. 5 in E Minor, Op. 64
(first theme)

5. Count in 2: Compound duple meter.

MEXICAN HAT DANCE

continued...

D.C. al Fine

6. Count in 3: Compound triple meter.

MORNING HAS BROKEN

Eleanor Farjeon
(England, 1881–1945)

Gaelic melody

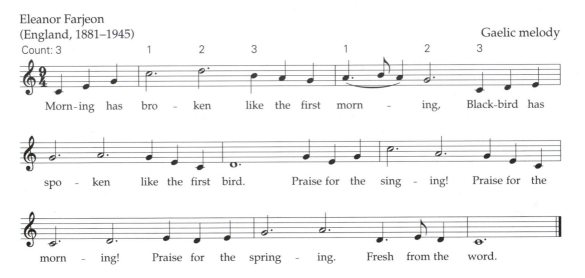

7. Count in 4: Compound quadruple meter.

NOCTURNE IN E-FLAT MAJOR, OP. 9, NO. 2 (R-45)

Frédéric Chopin
(Poland, 1810–1849)

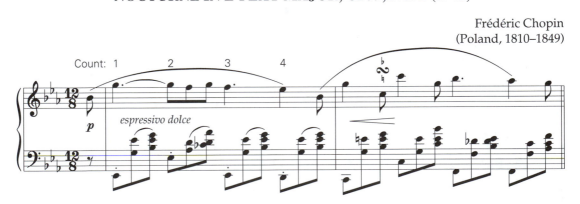

Listen to **Akan Music (R-46)** from Ghana, West Africa. Can you discern the basic beats in groups of twos? Are the divisions and subdivisions in twos or threes?

PRACTICE

Writing Meter Signatures (Time Signatures)

Complete this chart of time signatures. For each one, translate into beats per measure and beat units as shown in the first example.

SIMPLE METERS

Simple Duple	Simple Triple	Simple Quadruple
2\2	?	?
8\♩	8	8
?	?	4
4	4	4
?	3	?
2	2	2

COMPOUND METERS

Compound Duple	Compound Triple	Compound Quadruple
6\2	?	12
16\♪.	16	16
?	9	?
8	8	8
?	?	?
4	4	4

Duplets and Borrowed Division

A *duplet* results when a note in compound meter is subdivided as though it were in simple meter. This is called a *borrowed division.* In a duplet, you are fitting two notes into the time normally given to three.

This is the normal division:

$$\text{♩.} = \text{♫♪}$$

These are *duplets:*

$$\text{♩.} = \overset{2}{\text{♫}}$$

$$\text{♩.} = \overset{\lceil 2 \rceil}{\text{♩ ♩}}$$

Observe that where there is no beam, a bracket is used over the notes to show which notes belong to the duplet figure.

PRACTICE

Counting and Listening to Duplets

With your classmates, tap and count these rhythm exercises that include duplets. Use simple-meter syllables to count duplets in compound meter.

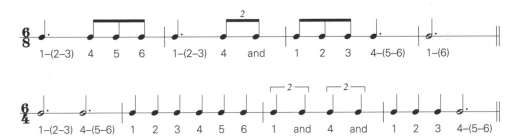

SECOND MOVEMENT
from Quartet No. 1 in G Minor, Op. 10
(first theme B)

Claude Debussy
(France, 1862—1918

mm. 9—16

PRACTICE

Writing Time Signatures and Phrases in Compound Meter

1. Put in the correct time signature for each line of notation.

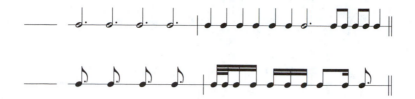

2. Write four measures after each time signature, using the counting numbers as a guide.

1–(2–3)	4–(5–6)		1–(2–3)	4	5	6	1	2	ee	3	4	and	1–(2–3–4–5–6)
Beats: 1	2		1	2			1	2					1	2

1–(2–3)	4–(5–6)		1–(2)	3	4–(5)	6	1	ee	2	ee	3	ee	4–(5)	6	1–(2–3–4–5–6)
Beats: 1	2		1		2		1						2		1	2

1–(2–3)	4–(5–6)	7–(8–9)	1–(2–3)	4	ee	5	ee	6	7–(8–9)	1	and	4–(5–6)	7–(8–9)	1	2	3	4–(5–6)	7–(8–9)
Beats: 1	2	3	1	2					3	1		2	3	1			2	3

SYNCOPATION

Syncopation results when an accent falls on a normally unaccented beat. This shifting of emphasis creates a feeling of energy in music and is a major feature in many types and eras of music. Syncopation is particularly evident in African and Latin American music. Our ears have grown accustomed to its influence on jazz, blues, ragtime, and rock.

PRACTICE

Reading and Clapping Syncopated Rhythms

With your instructor's assistance, clap these patterns. Pay careful attention to the accents.

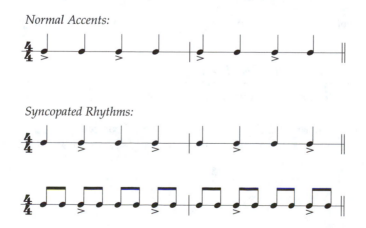

Normal Accents:

Syncopated Rhythms:

Listen to "Tom Dooley" as it is sung or played for you. Then tap the following rhythms, one without the syncopation and one showing the shifting accent.

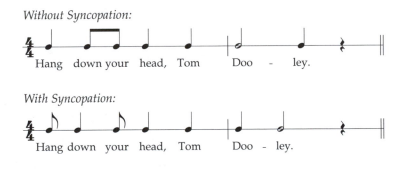

Without Syncopation:

Hang   down your   head,   Tom   Doo - ley.

With Syncopation:

Hang down   your   head,   Tom   Doo - ley.

TOM DOOLEY

Count: 1 & (2) & 3 4   U.S.A.

Hang down your head, Tom   Doo - ley,   Hang down your head and   cry.

Hang down your head, Tom   Doo - ley,   Poor boy, you're bound to   die.

MUSICAL APPLICATION

Singing Syncopated Rhythms

Find the syncopated rhythms in each song. Practice saying the syncopated lyrics under the bracketed notes while your foot taps steady beats. Then sing the songs with your class.

BLUES FOR YESTERDAY

Leonard Feather
Jane Feather

I've got the Blues For Yes-ter-day, it keeps on haunt-ing me _____

_____ I've got the Blues For Yes-ter-day, it keeps on haunt-ing me _____

_____ I've got the blues deep down _ for the days that used to be. _____

FUNGA ALAFIA

Liberian Welcome Dance

Fun-ga   A - la - fia   Ah-shay Ah-shay   Fun-ga   A - la - fia   Ah-shay Ah-shay

CAMPTOWN RACES

Stephen Foster
(United States, 1826–1864)

The Camp-town la - dies sing this song,   Doo - dah!   Doo - dah!   The
Oh see those hor - ses round the bend,   Doo - dah!   Doo - dah!   The

Camp-town race - track five miles long,   Oh,   Doo - dah   day!
Guess that race will nev - er end,   Oh,   Doo - dah   day!

Chorus

Goin'   to run   all   night!   Goin'   to run   all   day!   I'll ___

bet   my mon-ey on a bob - tail nag,   Some - bod - y bet on the bay.

CHE CHE KOOLAY

West African Ghana Folk Song

Call:
Cheh cheh kool - ay.

Response:
Cheh cheh kool - ay.

1 &-(2) & 3 4
Cheh cheh koh - fee sah.

Cheh cheh koh - fee sah. Kah - fee sah lang - ah. Kah - fee sah - lang - ah.

Tah-tah shee lahn - gah. Tah-tah shee lahn - ga. Coom ah-dye - day. Coom ah-dye - day.

EPO I TAI TAI E

Maori Song (New Zealand)

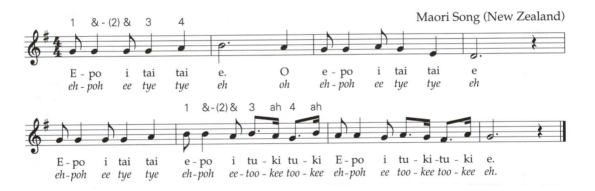

1 &-(2) & 3 4
E - po i tai tai e.
eh - poh ee tye tye eh

O e - po i tai tai e
oh eh - poh ee tye tye eh

1 &-(2) & 3 ah 4 ah
E - po i tai tai e - po i tu - ki tu - ki E - po i tu - ki-tu - ki e.
eh-poh ee tye tye eh-poh ee-too - kee too - kee eh-poh ee too - kee too - kee eh.

ARTZA ALINU

Israeli Dance Song

1 &-(2) & 3 4
Ar-tza a - li - nu, ar-tza a - li - nu, ar-tza a - li - nu.

Ar-tza a - li - nu. Ar-tza a - li - nu, ar-tza a - li - nu.

Translation: "We have found our land."

SOMETIMES I FEEL LIKE A MOTHERLESS CHILD

Black American Spiritual

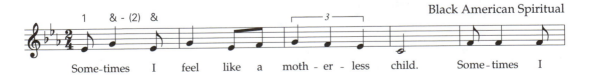

1 & - (2) & 3
Some-times I feel like a moth - er - less child. Some-times I

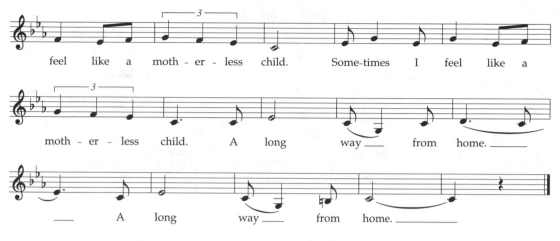

feel like a moth-er-less child. Some-times I feel like a

moth-er-less child. A long way from home.

A long way from home.

2. Sometimes I feel like I'm almost gone, [*three times*]
   A long way from home, a long way from home.

3. Sometimes I feel that the night is long, [*three times*]
   A long way from home, a long way from home.

4. Sometimes I feel that I haven't a friend, [*three times*]
   A long way from home, a long way from home.

LA RASPA

Mexican Folk Song

The work of the day is done. And un-der the set-ting sun. Their

mu-sic is bright and gay. Just hear those mu-si-cians play! The

voic-es are sing-ing a hap-py song. This is fi-es-ta day. And

peo-ple are glad that the night is long. This is the time to play!

MUSICAL APPLICATION

Listening to Syncopated Rhythms

Each of the following works includes syncopation. Locate the syncopated passages in the score excerpts before hearing the music.

PRELUDE III

George Gershwin
(United States, 1898–1937)

RAJASTHAN FOLK MELODY

North India

THE EASY WINNERS (R-47)

Scott Joplin
(United States, 1868–1917)

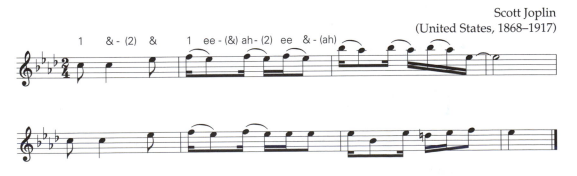

PRACTICE
Reading and Writing Syncopation

Listen to "Royal Garden Blues." Study the rhythmic notation, and locate the examples of syncopation. Write the counting numbers of the rhythm under the examples before discussing your answers with your group. Tap out the rhythm and hum the tune of the song.

ROYAL GARDEN BLUES

Clarence and Spencer Williams

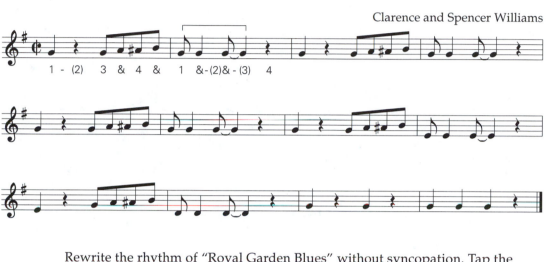

1 - (2)   3 & 4 &   1 &-(2)&-(3)   4

Rewrite the rhythm of "Royal Garden Blues" without syncopation. Tap the rhythm both with and without syncopation.

_____

_____

_____

Rewrite each line to include a syncopation.

_____

_____

_____

MUSICAL APPLICATION

Playing Syncopations in a Rock Accompaniment

Perform this rock accompaniment with a group of your classmates. The cymbal and the snare drum provide the syncopated effect. One performer can improvise a solo on the black keys of a piano while the accompaniment is played.

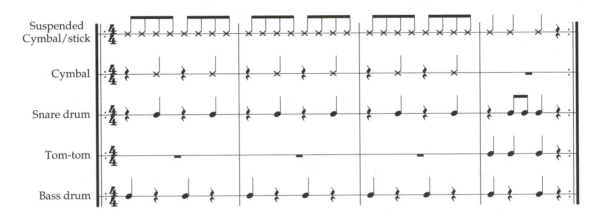

IRREGULAR RHYTHMIC ORGANIZATION

Asymmetric Meters

Asymmetric meters, which highlight irregular accents and uneven numbers of beats within a measure, are often used by twentieth-century composers and are found frequently in the music of the Balkan countries. Two common asymmetric meters are those with five and seven beats per measure. In each meter, the accents may be assigned two ways. Clap the following examples with your group.

MUSICAL APPLICATION

Listening to Music with Asymmetric Meters

Listen to the following instrumental works, which feature asymmetrical meters. The first has an uneven number of beats per measure; the second has irregular accents with eight beats grouped as 3 + 3 + 2.

FIRST MOVEMENT
from Symphony No. 1
(excerpt)

Howard Hanson
(United States, 1896–1991)

SIX DANCES IN BULGARIAN RHYTHM, No. 6
from *Mikrokosmos*, Book VI

Béla Bartók
(Hungary, 1881–1945)

MUSICAL APPLICATION

Singing a Song in an Asymmetric Meter

Step and clap this rhythm as you sing "Ta Kalotykha Vouna."

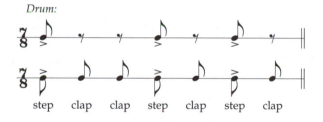

step clap clap step clap step clap

TA KALOTYKHA VOUNA

Edited and translated by
Nicholas M. England

Greek Folk Song from Thessaly
Collected and transcribed by Ellen Frye

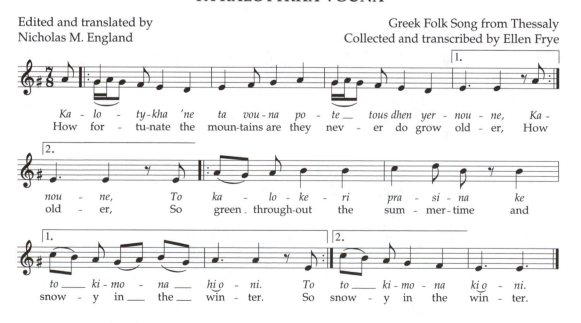

Ka - lo - ty-kha 'ne ta vou-na po - te __ tous dhen yer - nou - ne, Ka -
How for - tu-nate the moun-tains are they nev - er do grow old - er, How

nou - ne, To ka - lo - ke - ri pra - si - na ke
old - er, So green _ through-out the sum - mer-time and

to __ ki - mo - na __ hi_o - ni. To to __ ki - mo - na kio - ni.
snow - y in __ the __ win - ter. So snow - y in the win - ter.

Shifting or Mixed Meters

Shifting or *mixed meters* are found in compositions in which the composers change meters within a section or movement. Practice reading the following excerpt by counting aloud and tapping the rhythm with your classmates.

SECOND MOVEMENT (R-48)
from Quartet No. 1 in D, Op. 11

Peter I. Tchaikovsky
(Russia, 1840–1893)

MUSICAL APPLICATION

Listening to Shifting Meters

PRELUDE, Op. 11, No. 24   (R49)
(excerpt)

Alexander Scriabin
(Russia, 1872—1914

Twentieth-century composer Aaron Copland is noted for his use of rhythmic irregularity, shifting accents, and mixed meters. Can you tap the bass notes with your left hand and keep the five/four meters going with your right hand?

MEXICAN DANCE AND FINALE
from *Billy the Kid*
(excerpt)

Aaron Copland
(United States, 1900–1992)

MUSICAL APPLICATION

Singing a Song in Shifting Meters

Keep a steady quarter-note beat as you move from $\frac{4}{4}$ to $\frac{3}{4}$ and back to $\frac{4}{4}$.

SHENANDOAH

Virginia

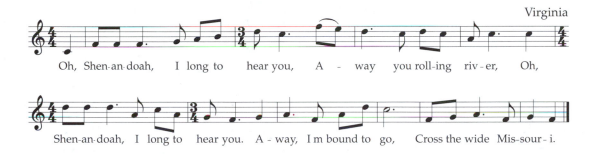

Oh, Shen-an-doah, I long to hear you, A - way you roll-ing riv - er, Oh,

Shen-an-doah, I long to hear you. A - way, I m bound to go, Cross the wide Mis-sour - i.

REVIEW OF TERMS

Define each term. Where appropriate, draw, notate, or use in a musical context to demonstrate your understanding.

1. compound meter
2. compound duple meter
3. compound triple meter
4. compound quadruple meter
5. duplet
6. borrowed division
7. syncopation
8. asymmetric meters
9. shifting meters

WORKSHEET
Chapter 6 Review

1. Write the time signatures for simple duple, simple triple, and simple quadruple meters. Notate two measures in each meter.

2. Write the time signatures for compound duple, compound triple, and compound quadruple meters. Notate two measures in each meter.

3. Write the counting numbers and syllables in compound meter for each example below.

4. Notate one measure in each meter to show the difference between accents and groupings in simple and compound meters. Use eighth notes.

$\frac{3}{4}$

$\frac{6}{8}$

5. Rewrite this phrase, replacing each group of three eighth notes with a duplet. Write the counting numbers under the new notes; then count aloud while tapping the rhythm.

6. Write a rhythm that illustrates shifting meters.

7. Put a bracket over the notes that include syncopation.

8. Put accents under selected notes to create or emphasize syncopated rhythms.

9. Listen as your instructor plays rhythms in simple and compound meters. Write an appropriate time signature for each one.

     a. _____

     b. _____

     c. _____

     d. _____

     e. _____

10. Write out an eight-measure example in $\frac{5}{4}$ meter. Use accent marks to indicate your grouping within each measure.

CHAPTER PROJECTS

1. Create 8-measure phrases in these compound meters.

$$\frac{6}{8} \qquad \frac{12}{8} \qquad \frac{6}{4} \qquad \frac{9}{8}$$

Remember to include tempo and dynamic markings. Work with a small group to count and tap the exercises.

2. Locate nineteenth-century American "rags." Find examples of syncopation in them.

3. Find an advertising jingle or verse in compound meter. Notate its rhythm.

4. Listen to *Nights in the Gardens of Spain,* by Manuel de Falla. What is the meter of the first movement?

5. Conduct your class in singing "Morning Has Broken," p. 144. (See Appendix B for conducting patterns.)

6. In Bali, complex rhythms are learned by rote and are never notated. The Kotekan is an intricate, flowing ceremonial rhythmic performance. With your classmates in two groups, try to read this two-part piece. Count each rhythm's numbers first; then say the chant in rhythm. Finally, transfer the rhythm to wood blocks, claves, or drums. Decide on a tempo for your performance, and change the dynamic level for each of the five repetitions.

KOTEKAN

Balinese Ceremonial Rhythm

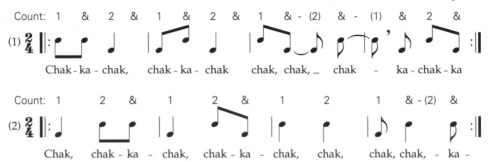

Count: 1 & 2 & 1 & 2 & 1 & - (2) & - (1) & 2 &

(1) Chak - ka - chak, chak - ka - chak chak, chak, _ chak - ka - chak - ka

Count: 1 2 & 1 2 & 1 2 1 & - (2) &

(2) Chak, chak - ka - chak, chak - ka - chak, chak, chak, chak, - ka -

Modes and Other Scale Patterns

The major and minor scales you have learned are the foundation of most Western music composed since about 1600. Music from earlier periods is based on different scales, called *modes,* and may be challenging to you because of its unfamiliar melodic sources. Similarly, most of the world's music, based on a myriad of scales, may seem to lack "tunes" or be unsingable. As you become knowledgeable about other scale patterns, you will open the door to the understanding and enjoyment of early Western and global musics.

MODES (CHURCH MODES)

From about 500 to about 1600—the Medieval and Renaissance periods of the Western world—six scales, or *modes* (also called *church modes*), were in common use. Two of the six modes, the Ionian and the Aeolian, survive as our present-day major and minor scales. Some of the others have returned in the nineteenth and twentieth centuries as modern composers have experimented with "new" scale patterns and have used modal folk melodies in their larger works.

When we compare the modes with major and minor scales, we find that the Ionian and Aeolian modes are identical to the major and natural minor scales, respectively. The remaining modes, with one alteration each, are like either major or natural minor scales. The Locrian, a theoretical scale not used in common practice, is not included in this group.

You can hear the patterns of half steps and whole steps in the church modes by playing on the white keys of a keyboard instrument.

MUSICAL APPLICATION

Playing Modes on the White Keys of a Keyboard

Play the modes on a keyboard. Observe the placement of half steps and whole steps in each one.

Ionian (major)

 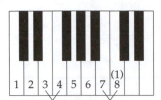

Dorian (natural minor
with raised 6th)

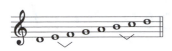 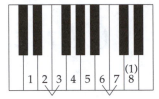

Phrygian (natural minor
with flatted 2nd)

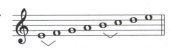 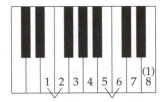

Lydian (major with
raised 4th)

 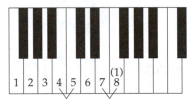

Mixolydian (major with
flatted 7th)

 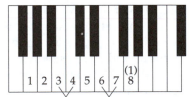

Aeolian (natural minor)

Locrian (natural minor,
flatted 2nd and 5th)

 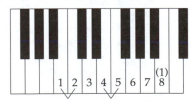

MUSICAL APPLICATION

Singing Modal Songs

You can learn to recognize modal music when you hear it. The following selections are examples of modal music featuring the Dorian and Mixolydian modes. Hum the tones of each song's modal scale before you sing it with your classmates. Mark the notes in the song that determine that its mode is neither major nor minor.

DORIAN MODE ON D

NOËL NOUVELET

SCARBOROUGH FAIR

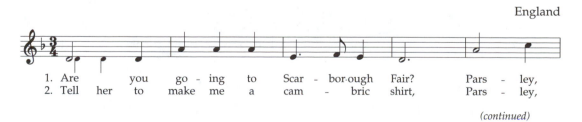

(continued)

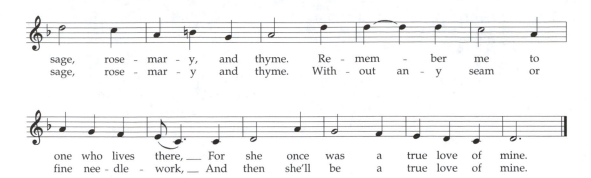

sage,   rose - mar - y,   and   thyme.   Re - mem - ber   me   to
sage,   rose - mar - y   and   thyme.   With - out   an - y   seam   or

one   who   lives   there, __   For   she   once   was   a   true   love   of   mine.
fine   nee - dle - work, __   And   then   she'll   be   a   true   love   of   mine.

DORIAN MODE ON C

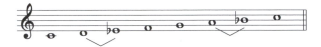

WHAT SHALL WE DO WITH THE DRUNKEN SAILOR?

American Sea Shanty

What shall we do with the drunk-en sai - lor,   *(Repeat)*

(Repeat)   Ear - ly   in   the   morn - ing?

MIXOLYDIAN MODE ON F

GOLDEN RING AROUND THE SUSAN GIRL
(excerpt)

Refrain   U.S.A.

'Round and a - round,   Su - san   girl,   'Round and a - round,   Su - san   girl,

'Round and a - round,   Su - san   girl,   All the way a - round,   Su - san   girl.

MIXOLYDIAN MODE ON D

OLD JOE CLARK

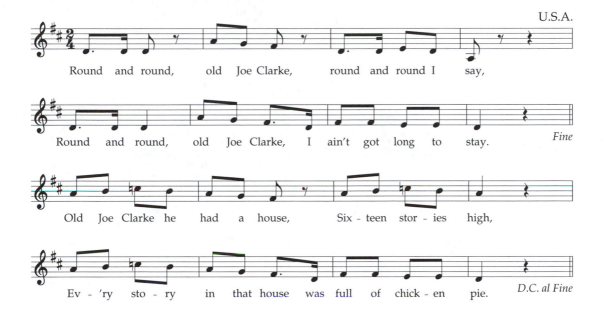

PRACTICE

Writing Modal Scales

Write the indicated modes. First show the notation for each mode corresponding to the white keys of a keyboard. Then write the mode beginning on another note, as indicated. Use accidentals to place half steps appropriately.

Dorian Mode

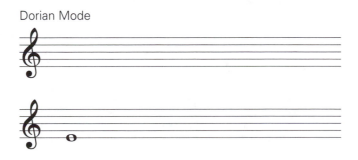

Phrygian Mode

Mixolydian Mode

Lydian Mode

MUSICAL APPLICATION

Listening to Modal Music

Four examples of modal instrumental pieces are shown here. Play the Lydian, Phrygian, and Mixolydian modal scales on a keyboard before listening to the musical examples.

LYDIAN MODE

MAZURKA, Op. 24, No. 2 (R-50)

Frédéric Chopin
(Poland, 1810–1849)

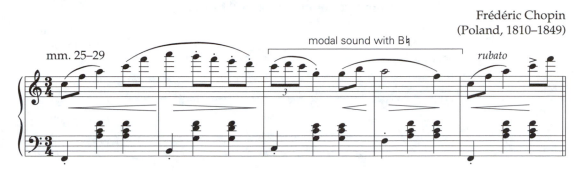

PHRYGIAN MODE

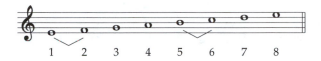

THIRD MODE MELODY

Thomas Tallis
(England, 1505–1585)

SECOND MOVEMENT (R-51)
from Symphony No. 4 in E Minor

Johannes Brahms
(Germany, 1833–1897)

MIXOLYDIAN MODE

FIRST MOVEMENT
from Symphony No. 3 ("A Pastoral Symphony")

Ralph Vaughan Williams
(England, 1872–1958)

THE PENTATONIC SCALE

The *pentatonic scale* (*penta*, "five"), a five-note pattern without half steps, is found in various forms in folk music throughout the world. It is the basis for much American folk and spiritual music and is prevalent in Native American, Asian, and African music.

To learn the sound of the pentatonic scale, play the black keys on a keyboard.

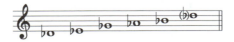

You can create a pentatonic scale starting on the tonic note of any major scale and using the following pattern. Any tone in a pentatonic scale could be the tonic.

Degrees of F major: 1   2   3   5   6

The fourth and seventh degrees of the major scale are omitted in this pattern, thereby eliminating half steps. Thus, the tones of this scale sounded randomly together do not create dissonances but, rather, "pleasant," consonant sounds. Pentatonic songs can be accompanied by drones, or borduns, created by sounding simultaneously the tonic (first scale degree) and the dominant (fifth scale degree) of the pentaton associated with the song.

MUSICAL APPLICATION

Singing Pentatonic Songs

Study the pentatonic scales associated with these songs. Ask a classmate to sound the drone for each song on its beats using a keyboard.

Pentatonic scale on F: Play the notes of this scale. Write the scale numbers over the notes of the song. Then accompany the song with a drone on F and C while singing.

1   2   3   5   6   Drones

TONGO

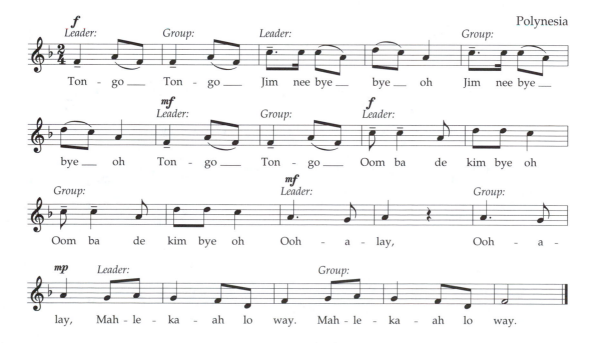

"Auld Lang Syne" appears here in F pentatonic. Accompany the song with a drone on F and C.

AULD LANG SYNE

Scotland

Should auld ac-quaint-ance be for-got, And nev - er brought to mind? Should

auld   ac-quaint - ance   be   for - got,   And   days   of   auld   lang   syne?

Chorus

For   auld ___ lang ___ syne,   my dear,   For   auld ___ lang ___ syne;   We'll

take   a   cup   of   kind - ness yet   for   auld ___ lang ___ syne.

Pentatonic scale on E-flat: Study the E-flat pentatonic scale. Write the scale numbers over the notes in the song. Then sing the song and accompany it with a drone.

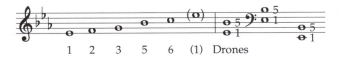

1   2   3   5   6   (1)   Drones

SOURWOOD MOUNTAIN

U.S.A.

Chick-ens crow-ing on   Sour-wood Moun-tain;   Hey   de ing dang   dil-ly dal-ly day.

So   ma - ny pret-ty girls   I   can't count them;   Hey   de ing dang   dil-ly dal-ly day.

PRACTICE

Writing Pentatonic Scales

Write the pentatonic scale associated with each song.

ALL GOD'S CHILDREN GOT SHOES

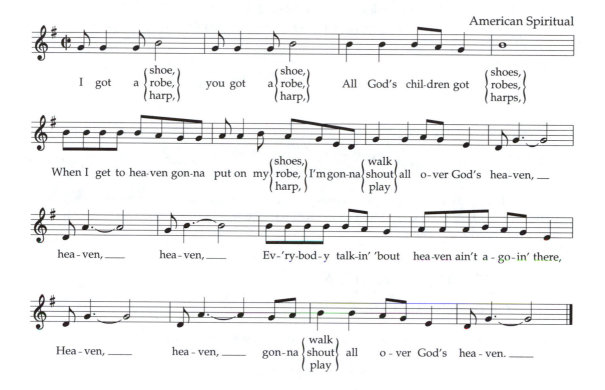

American Spiritual

I got a {shoe, robe, harp,} you got a {shoe, robe, harp,} All God's chil-dren got {shoes, robes, harps,}

When I get to hea-ven gon-na put on my {shoes, robe, harp,} I'm gon-na {walk shout play} all o-ver God's hea-ven, ___

hea-ven, ___ hea-ven, ___ Ev-'ry-bod-y talk-in' 'bout hea-ven ain't a-go-in' there,

Hea-ven, ___ hea-ven, ___ gon-na {walk shout play} all o-ver God's hea-ven. ___

THAT GREAT GETTING UP MORNING
(excerpt)

American Spiritual

In that great get-ting up morn-ing fare you well, ___ fare you well, ___ In that

great get-ting up morn - ing fare you well, ___ fare you well, ___

THE WHOLE-TONE SCALE

The *whole-tone scale* is made up of six whole steps. Because all the tones are the same distance apart, music based on this scale has a distinctive quality, with no tonic or tonal center of gravity. Whole-tone music, lacking movement toward a tonic conclusion, gives an impression of indecision. The composers who achieved this sound in their music are called *impressionists.* Included among the impressionists of the late nineteenth century are Claude Debussy (1862–1918), Maurice Ravel (1875–1937), and Charles Griffes (1884–1920).

There are two whole-tone scales. Play them on a piano.

Now, play them again, this time pressing down on the damper (rightmost) pedal as you play. The blending of the tones in the whole-tone scale will result in the impressionists' sound.

MUSICAL APPLICATION

Listening to Whole-Tone Music

Play the whole-tone scale passages in this work before listening to it.

WHOLE-TONE SCALE

PRELUDE (R-52)
from *Voiles* (Veils), Book I, No. 2

Claude Debussy
(France, 1862–1918)

THE BLUES SCALE

The *blues* has been the most important influence on the development of Western popular music since the 1940s. The blues is the basis for much of the rhythm and blues, jazz styles, and pop music of today. Blues music has the effect of wailing because the performer flattens certain tones of the diatonic major scale. In the blue melodies, the third and seventh scale degrees are flatted.

Play this blues scale on a piano.

MUSICAL APPLICATION

Sing "St. Louis Blues," a song that is distinctive because the third degree of the scale is flatted.

ST. LOUIS BLUES
(excerpt)

W. C. Handy
(United States, 1873—1958

The blues chord progression to accompany this song appears on p. 241.

REVIEW OF TERMS

Define each term. Where appropriate, notate or use in a musical context to demonstrate your understanding.

1. mode
2. Ionian mode
3. Aeolian mode
4. Dorian mode
7. Mixolydian mode
8. pentatonic scale
9. drone, bordun
10. whole-tone scale

WORKSHEET
Chapter 7 Review

1. The major and minor scales are derived from two modes, the _____ and the _____.

2. From about 500 to about 1600, six scales, called modes, were in common use They are

a. _____   d. _____

b. _____   e. _____

c. _____   f. _____

3. Modal scales can be played on the white keys of a piano for quick identification of half- and whole-step patterns. Which mode begins on each key?

a. C _____   d. F _____

b. D _____   e. G _____

c. E _____   f. A _____

4. Which three of the six commonly used modes resemble major scales with two whole steps at the beginning?

a. _____

b. _____

c. _____

5. Which two modes resemble minor scales with a whole step and a half step at the beginning?

a. _____

b. _____

6. Notate a pentatonic scale.

7. Which scale degrees of a major scale make up a pentatonic scale?

_____

8. A drone is made up of which two scale degrees from a pentatonic scale?

_____

9. Notate the two whole-tone scales.

10. Music based on a whole-tone scale lacks movement toward a

_____

11. Composers who used the whole-tone scales in the late nineteenth century were

known as _____

12. Describe the sound, or affect, of whole-tone music.

_____

13. Notate a blues scale beginning on middle C.

CHAPTER PROJECTS

1. In the blank next to the title, write the name of the minor scale or the mode that is associated with each of these songs.

MAM'ZELLE ZIZI

_____

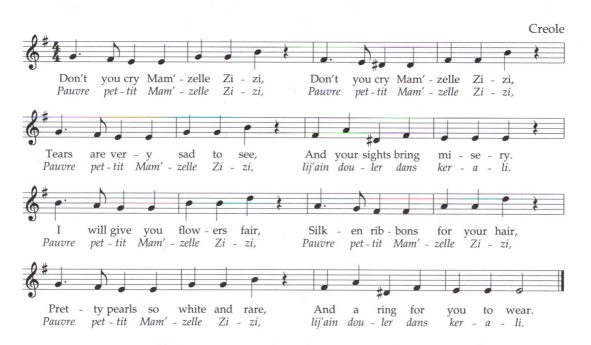

Creole

Don't   you cry Mam' - zelle   Zi - zi,   Don't   you cry Mam' - zelle   Zi - zi,
Pauvre   pet - tit   Mam' - zelle   Zi - zi,   Pauvre   pet - tit   Mam' - zelle   Zi - zi,

Tears   are ver - y   sad   to   see,   And   your sights bring   mi - se - ry.
Pauvre   pet - tit   Mam' - zelle   Zi - zi,   lij'ain dou - ler   dans   ker - a - li.

I   will give   you   flow - ers   fair,   Silk - en rib - bons   for   your hair,
Pauvre   pet - tit   Mam' - zelle   Zi - zi,   Pauvre   pet - tit   Mam' - zelle   Zi - zi,

Pret - ty pearls so   white and rare,   And   a   ring for   you   to   wear.
Pauvre   pet - tit   Mam' - zelle   Zi - zi,   lij'ain dou - ler   dans   ker - a - li.

MY LAST FAREWELL TO STIRLING

_____

Australian Folk Song

Nae lark   in trans - port mounts the sky,   Nor_ leaves with ear - ly plain - tive cry,   But

I   maun bid _ my   last   good - bye, _   My   last   fare - well _   to   Stir - ling O.

From *The Penguin Book of Australian Folk Songs* by John Manifold, The Dominion Press, North Blackburn, Victoria, Australia, 19

AS I ROVED OUT

Newfoundland

As I roved out one fine sum-mer's eve - ning, To view the flowers and to take the _ air, 'Twas

there I spied a ten - der _ moth - er, Talk - in' to her _ daugh - ter _ fair.

2. A sailor boy thinks all for to wander,
And he will prove your overthrow.
O daughter, you're better to wed with a farmer,
For to sea he'll never go.

2. Work with a small group to sing or play "St. Louis Blues" (p. 173) in C major without the "blue" notes. Then sing the song *with* the blue notes. Describe the affect of each version.

3. Find a pentatonic American spiritual or folk song. Bring it to class and work with another student to sing it and accompany it with a drone.

4. Locate a score and a recording of Ferruccio Busoni's *Sonatina Seconda* (1912). Find whole-tone passages for the right hand. Listen to the recording.

5. Listen to the following orchestral work. Compare it with Tallis's "Third Mode Melody" (Phrygian) on p. 167.

FANTASIA ON A THEME BY THOMAS TALLIS (R-53)

Ralph Vaughn Williams
(England, 1872–1958)

CHAPTER **8**

Intervals

Intervals could be called the building blocks of melody, for a melody is made up of a series of pitches and *an interval is the distance between two musical pitches.* The ability to sight-read these distances and to "hear" them when looking at a musical score is considered a necessity in the preparation of most professional musicians. Amateurs who want to enjoy the independence that derives from good sight-reading ability find that knowing intervallic distances helps them read melodies readily.

INTERVAL SIZE NAMES: NUMERICAL IDENTIFICATION

Melodic Intervals

We shall begin our work with intervals by looking at the size of *melodic* intervals, or distances between two pitches sounded one after the other. We determine the size of an interval by counting letters of the musical alphabet in moving from one pitch to the next. Study the following intervals and locate them on your keyboard.

Unisons: Identical pitches (also called *primes*).

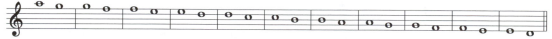

Seconds: Count 2 letters, including the first one.

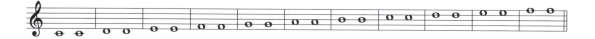

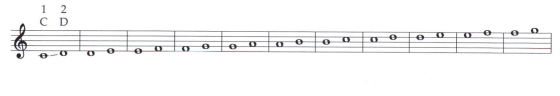

177

Thirds: Count 3 letters, including the first one.

1 2 3
C D E

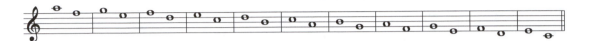

Fourths: Count 4 letters, including the first one.

1 2 3 4
C D E F

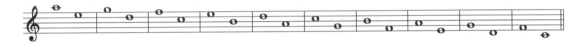

Fifths: Count 5 letters, including the first one.

1 2 3 4 5
C D E F G

Sixths: Count 6 letters, including the first one.

1 2 3 4 5 6
C D E F G A

Sevenths: Count 7 letters, including the first one.

1 2 3 4 5 6 7
C D E F G A B

Octaves (8ve): Identical letters; count 8 letters, including the first one.

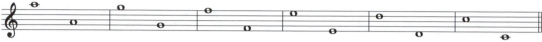

Visual Assistance in Identifying Intervals

Go back and study again the examples of intervals, keeping in mind these rules about their appearance:

1. Unisons, or *primes,* appear on the same line or space.
2. Seconds are always on adjacent lines or spaces.
3. *Both* pitches in thirds, fifths, and sevenths appear on either spaces or lines.
4. Fourths and sixths place one pitch on a space, the other on a line.
5. An octave has eight scale degrees, beginning and ending with notes of the same letter name. It may also be measured as twelve half steps.
6. Distances in the bass and C clefs are measured in the same way as distances in the G, or treble, clef.

PRACTICE

Numerical Identification of Intervals

What is the intervallic distance in each set of pitches? Write the numerical names (unison, 2nd, 3rd, 4th, 5th, and so on). The first one is done for you.

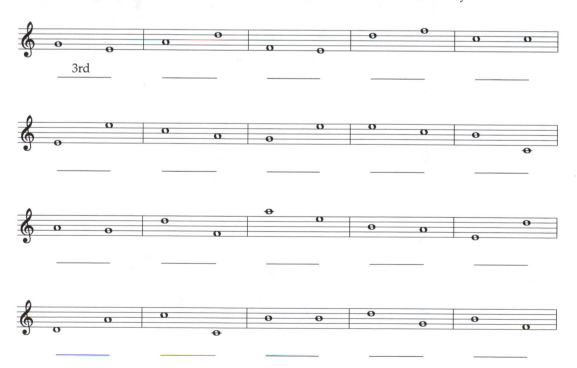

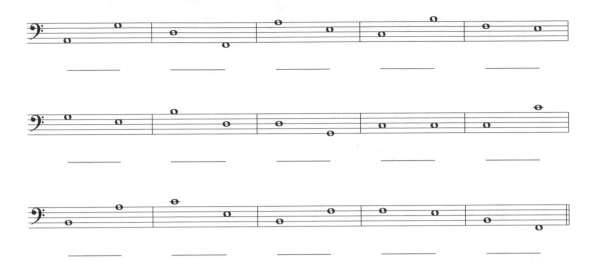

PRACTICE

Notating and Naming Intervals

1. In these intervals, the second pitch is *higher* than the first. Write the numerical name of each interval. Then notate it on the staff. The first one is done for you.

a. C–D   2nd

b. A–F   ____

c. E–A   ____

d. G–D   ____

e. D–C   ____

f. C–C   ____

g. F–A   ____

h. D–A   ____

i. B–E   ____

j. C–A   ____

2. In these intervals, the second pitch is *lower* than the first. Notate each one on the staff. Then write the numerical names of the intervals. The first one is done for you.

a. G–E   3rd

f. D–A _____

b. A–C _____

g. A–A _____

c. F–E _____

h. G–F _____

d. C–F _____

i. C–G _____

e. B–C _____

j. B–D _____

Harmonic Intervals

When the tones of an interval sound simultaneously, the interval is *harmonic*. The intervallic distances of harmonic intervals are measured in the same way as those of melodic intervals. You will need to know harmonic intervals to learn about triads and chords. Study the following harmonic intervals.

Unisons, or primes:

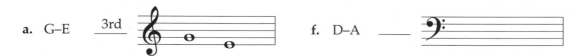

Seconds:

Thirds:

Fourths:

Fifths:

Sixths:

Sevenths:

Octaves:

PRACTICE

Numerical Identification of Harmonic Intervals

Identify the intervallic distances of these harmonic intervals. The first one is done for you.

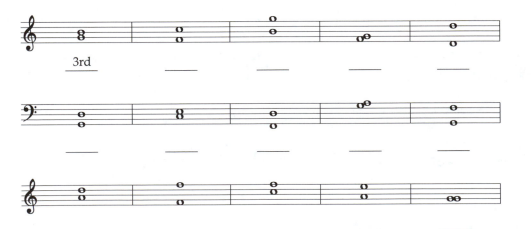

PRACTICE

Writing Harmonic Intervals

Write harmonic intervals above each numerical identification. The lower pitch of each interval is notated.

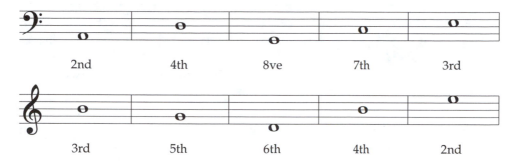

| 2nd | 4th | 8ve | 7th | 3rd |

| 3rd | 5th | 6th | 4th | 2nd |

INTERVAL QUALITY NAMES

Perfect and Major Intervals (Diatonic Intervals)

We have been working with numerical identification of intervals—determining the distance between two pitches. An interval is also identified by its characteristic sound, or quality. Two terms, *perfect* and *major,* signify that *the upper tone of an interval is in the major scale of the lower tone.* That interval is therefore a diatonic interval.

Perfect intervals are unisons, fourths, fifths, and octaves. Major intervals are seconds, thirds, sixths, and sevenths. When we identify intervals completely, *we combine the quality and numerical names.* Study these diatonic intervals in C major:

INTERVAL NAMES

Quality:	perfect	major	major	perfect	perfect	major	major	perfect
Size:	unison	second	third	fourth	fifth	sixth	seventh	octave

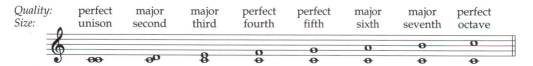

The numerical identification of perfect and major intervals can also be determined by counting the half steps between the notes.

Examples in C Major: C C♯ D D♯ E F F♯ G G♯ A A♯ B C

Interval	Letter Names	Half Steps
Perfect Unison	(C–C)	0
Major Second	(C–D)	2
Major Third	(C–E)	4
Perfect Fourth	(C–F)	5
Perfect Fifth	(C–G)	7
Major Sixth	(C–A)	9
Major Seventh	(C–B)	11
Perfect Octave	(C–C)	12

Study these diatonic intervals in G major. Note the abbreviations for quality and numerical names under each interval.

INTERVAL NAMES

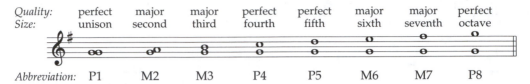

Quality:	perfect	major	major	perfect	perfect	major	major	perfect
Size:	unison	second	third	fourth	fifth	sixth	seventh	octave
Abbreviation:	P1	M2	M3	P4	P5	M6	M7	P8

The following diatonic intervals are written in F major. Identify each one using its quality and numerical abbreviations.

PRACTICE

Naming Intervals in D Major

Name these diatonic intervals in D major. Be sure to include both the quality and the numerical abbreviations.

a. _____ b. _____ c. _____ d. _____ e. _____ f. _____ g. _____

Which interval is missing in the example above? Write it here. Name it correctly.

h. _____

PRACTICE

Changing Harmonic Intervals to Melodic Intervals

Rewrite as melodic intervals the harmonic intervals shown in the preceding Practice. Then play both the harmonic and the melodic examples at a keyboard.

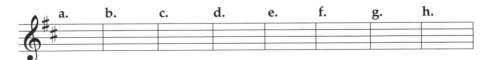

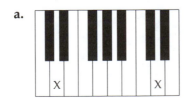

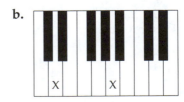

c.

f.

d.
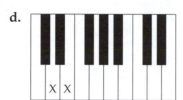

g.
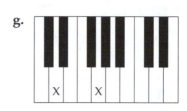

e.
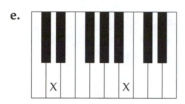

h.
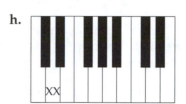

PRACTICE

Writing Major Intervals

Write in the *higher* pitch for each of these major intervals. Check your answer. Does the higher pitch fit into the major scale that begins on the lower pitch?

M2   M6   M7   M3   M7   M6

M3   M7   M2   M6   M3   M2

M7   M6   M3   M2   M6   M7

Write in the *lower* pitch for each of these major intervals. Check your answer. Does the higher pitch belong in the major scale of the lower pitch you selected? If not, you need to select another lower pitch. The first one is done for you.

M3   M7   M6   M7   M2   M3

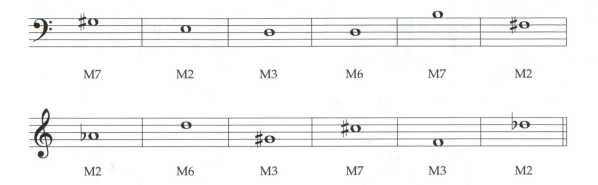

PRACTICE

Writing Perfect Intervals

The following intervals are perfect—P4, P5, or P8 as indicated. Write in the *higher* pitch. Check your answer by fitting the higher pitch into the major scale that begins on the lower pitch. The first one is done for you.

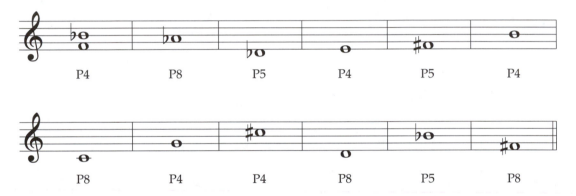

The following intervals are P4, P5, or P8 as indicated. Write in the *lower* pitch. Check your answer. Is the higher note included in the major scale that begins on the lower note? The first one is done for you.

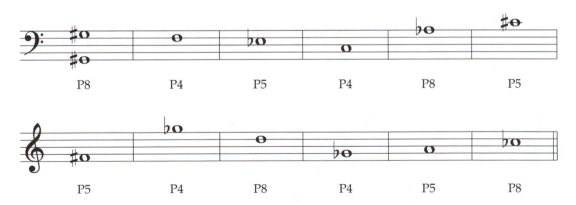

PRACTICE

Identifying Perfect and Major Intervals

Identify the following harmonic and melodic intervals by quality (P or M) and intervallic, or numerical, distance (1, 2, 3, 4, and so on). Begin by thinking of the lower note as the tonic of a major scale. Determine the numerical size of the interval by counting the notes included in it. Remember that the perfect intervals are unisons, fourths, fifths, and octaves. The major intervals are seconds, thirds, sixths, and sevenths. The first one is done for you.

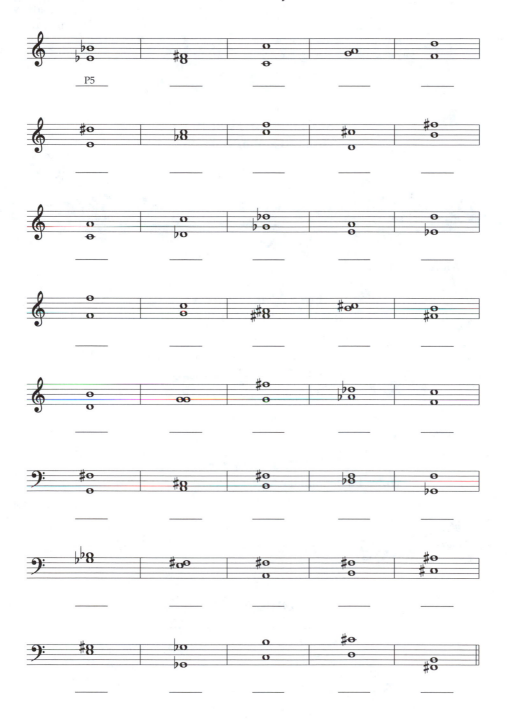

MUSICAL APPLICATION

Reading Major and Perfect Intervals in Music Literature

Listen as your instructor plays the following excerpts for you. Follow the score as you read each one.

Perfect Prime (Unison)

MARCH
from *Tannhäuser*, Act II

Richard Wagner
(Germany, 1813–1883)

Major Second

SECOND MOVEMENT
from Symphony No. 100

Franz Joseph Haydn
(Austria, 1732–1809)

Major Third

FIRST MOVEMENT
from Symphony No. 5, Op. 67

Ludwig van Beethoven
(Germany, 1770–1827)

Perfect Fourth

NOCTURNE
from *A Midsummer Night's Dream*, Op. 61, No. 7

Felix Mendelssohn
(Germany, 1809–1847)

OVERTURE
from *The Flying Dutchman*

Richard Wagner
(Germany, 1813–1883)

L'ÉLÉPHANT
from *Carnaval des Animaux*

Camille Saint-Saëns
(France, 1835–1921)

Perfect Fifth

THUS SPAKE ZARATHUSTRA

Richard Strauss
(Germany, 1864–1949)

FINALE
from Symphony No. 3, Op. 55

Ludwig van Beethoven
(Germany, 1770–1827)

Major Sixth

OVERTURE
from *Die Meistersinger*

Richard Wagner
(Germany, 1813–1883)

Major Seventh

INTRODUCTION AND RONDO CAPRICCIOSO, OP. 28
(third theme)

Camille Saint-Saëns
(France, 1835–1921)

Perfect Octave

THIRD MOVEMENT
from *Classical Symphony*

Sergei Prokofiev
(Russia, 1891–1953)

Augmented, Minor, and Diminished Intervals (Nondiatonic Intervals)

A *nondiatonic interval* is created when an interval is altered so that the upper note is not found in the major scale of the lower note. For example, the following intervals are all thirds, but they are not all of the same quality. Play them on a keyboard to hear the differences.

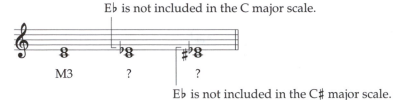

The following intervals are all sixths, but they are not all of the same quality. Study these examples.

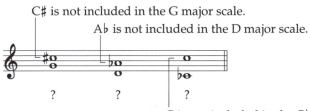

The following intervals appear to be perfect but are not of perfect quality. Their higher notes do not fit into the major scales of their lower notes.

Augmented Intervals   Both perfect and major intervals may be increased by one half step to become *augmented* intervals, indicated by the uppercase letter *A* or the sign +. Study the following examples. Observe that each major and perfect interval is followed by two augmented examples. The first of the augmented intervals is created by raising the interval's upper note by one half step; the second augmented interval is created by lowering the interval's lower note by one half step.

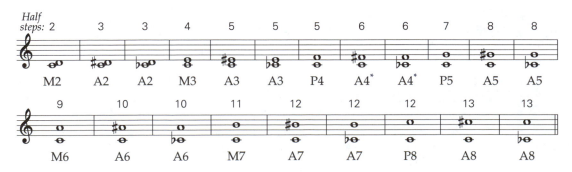

*A4 is called a *tritone*—three whole steps.

PRACTICE

Writing Perfect, Major, and Augmented Intervals

Add the higher note of each interval named below the staff. Remember that in perfect and major intervals, the lower note may be considered the tonic of a scale and the higher note must fit into that scale. To write an augmented interval, remember that it will be one half step larger than the major intervals (seconds, thirds, sixths, and sevenths) or the perfect intervals (unisons, fourths, fifths, and octaves). The first one is done for you.

A4   A6   P5   A2   M2   P1   A3   P8   A5   P4   A7   M6

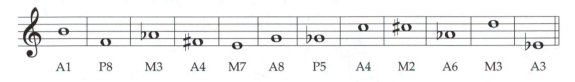

A1   P8   M3   A4   M7   A8   P5   A4   M2   A6   M3   A3

Add the lower note of each interval. Use the scale-check approach described above for major and perfect intervals. Be sure the lower note is the tonic of a scale that includes the upper note. If the interval is augmented, lower the tonic note one half step.

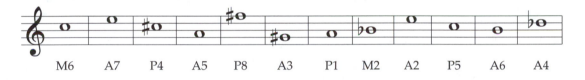

M6   A7   P4   A5   P8   A3   P1   M2   A2   P5   A6   A4

A3   M3   A6   M2   A4   M6   A8   M7   A4   M3   P8   A5

PRACTICE

Creating Augmented Intervals

The intervals shown here are major or perfect. Identify the intervals by numerical size and quality. Then rewrite them as augmented intervals. Observe that some are notated as melodic intervals.

_____   _____   _____   _____

Minor Intervals   A *minor* interval results when a major interval is reduced in size by one half step. The alteration may be to either the upper or the lower note of the interval. Minor intervals are indicated by a lowercase *m*. (Note: Perfect intervals *never* become minor.) Study these examples.

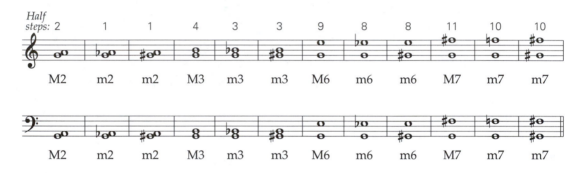

PRACTICE

Writing Major and Minor Intervals

Add the top note of each interval. Remember that in major intervals, the top note must be in the scale of the tonic indicated by the bottom note.

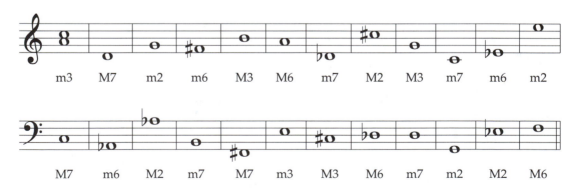

MUSICAL APPLICATION

Reading Minor Intervals in Music Literature

Listen as your instructor plays the following excerpts. Follow the score as you read each one.

Minor Second

VARIATIONS ON A THEME BY HAYDN, OP. 56a

Johannes Brahms
(Germany, 1833–1897)

FIRST MOVEMENT
from Symphony in D Minor

César Franck
(France, 1822–1890)

Minor Third

LULLABY

Johannes Brahms
(Germany, 1833–1897)

FINALE
from Symphony No. 3, Op. 55

Ludwig van Beethoven
(Germany, 1770–1827)

SECOND MOVEMENT
from Symphony No. 5 in E Minor

Antonin Dvořák
(Bohemia, 1841–1904)

Minor Sixth

FIRST MOVEMENT
from Symphony No. 5 in D, Op. 47

Dmitri Shostakovitch
(Russia, 1906–1975)

Minor Seventh

AN DER SCHÖNEN BLAUEN DONAU, OP. 317
(On the Beautiful Blue Danube)

Johann Strauss, Jr.
(Austria, 1825–1899)

ENIGMA VARIATIONS
(theme)

Sir Edward Elgar
(England, 1857–1934)

Diminished Intervals   A *diminished* interval is created by reducing the size of a perfect or a minor interval. Either the top note is lowered one half step, or the bottom note is raised one half step. The diminished interval is indicated by the lowercase letter *d* or by the sign °. Study these examples.

Half steps: 5   4   4   7   6   6   12   11   11

P4   d4   d4   P5   d5   d5   P8   d8   d8

3	2	2	8	7	7	10	9	9
m3	d3	d3	m6	d6	d6	m7	d7	d7

PRACTICE

Identifying Diminished Intervals

The following intervals are either perfect or diminished. Beneath each interval, write its identification, including numerical size and quality.

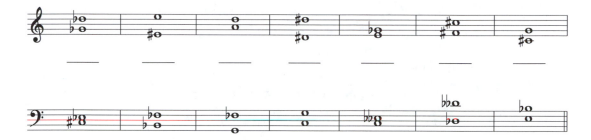

PRACTICE

Writing Diminished Intervals

Create two diminished intervals from each perfect interval shown here.

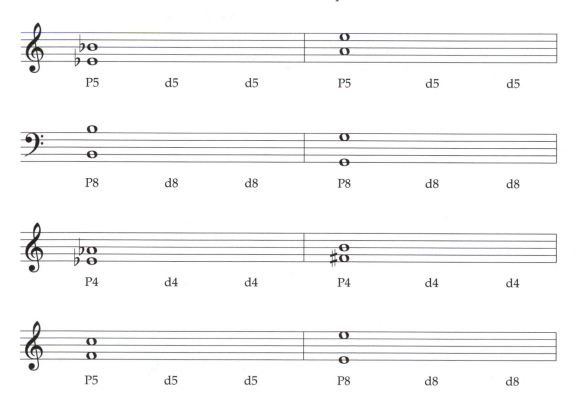

P5	d5	d5	P5	d5	d5

P8	d8	d8	P8	d8	d8

P4	d4	d4	P4	d4	d4

P5	d5	d5	P8	d8	d8

MUSICAL APPLICATION

Reading Augmented and Diminished Intervals in Music Literature

Read each excerpt at a keyboard.

Augmented Second and Fourth

SIXTH BAGATELLE

Béla Bartók
(Hungary, 1881–1945)

Augmented Fourth

SONATA, OP. 5, NO. 8

Arcangelo Corelli
(Italy, 1653–1713)

Augmented Sixth

MAZURKA, OP. 7, NO. 2

Frédéric Chopin
(Poland, 1810–1849)

Diminished Fourth and Fifth

TILL EULENSPIEGEL

Richard Strauss
(Germany, 1864–1949)

Diminished Fifth and Augmented Second

SONGS WITHOUT WORDS, OP. 19, NO. 2

Felix Mendelssohn
(Germany, 1809–1847)

Diminished Seventh

SONATA, K. 332

W. A. Mozart
(Austria, 1756–1791)

PRACTICE

Identifying Minor and Diminished Intervals

Review by studying these examples.

Minor Sixth: Major sixth reduced by one half step

Diminished Sixth: Major sixth reduced by one whole step

Diminished Fourth: Perfect fourth reduced by one half step

Determine the numerical size of each interval. Then identify its quality as minor (*m*) or diminished (*d*). Remember that major intervals become minor when they are reduced by a half step and diminished when they are reduced by a whole step. Perfect intervals do not become minor but are diminished when their size is reduced by one half step.

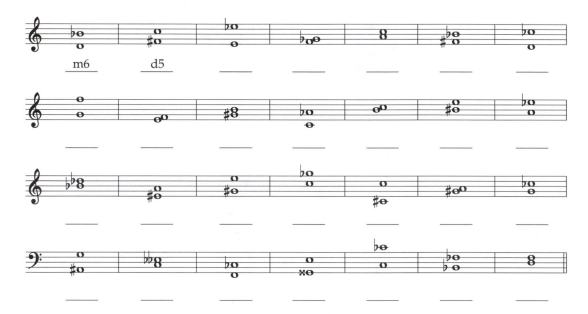

PRACTICE

Identifying Perfect, Augmented, and Diminished Intervals

These intervals include unisons, fourths, fifths, and octaves. Identify each one as P (perfect), A (augmented), or D (diminished).

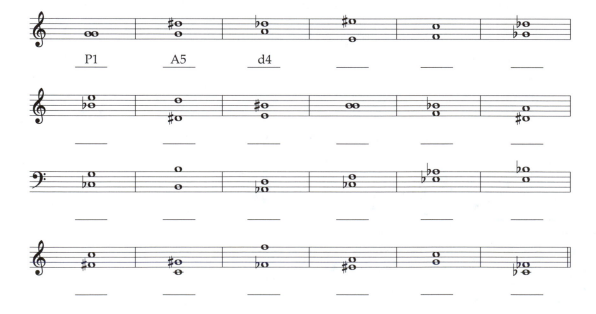

MUSICAL APPLICATION

Intervals in Songs

Practice singing the intervals in these song excerpts. Then move the first pitch of the bracketed notes to random places on the keyboard and sing the excerpts again.

Unison:

MAME

m2:

JOSHUA FOUGHT THE BATTLE OF JERICHO

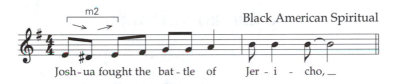

M2:

WE SHALL OVERCOME

m3:

THE CAISSONS GO ROLLING ALONG

M3:

SWING LOW, SWEET CHARIOT

P4:

I'VE BEEN WORKING ON THE RAILROAD

U.S.A. Folk Song

I've been work-ing on the rail - road, All the live-long day,

AMAZING GRACE

American Hymn Tune

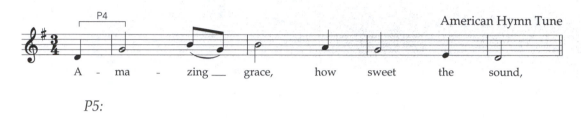

A - ma - zing ___ grace, how sweet the sound,

P5:

SCARBOROUGH FAIR

England

Are you go - ing to Scar - bo - rough Fair? _____

m6:

LET MY PEOPLE GO

Spiritual

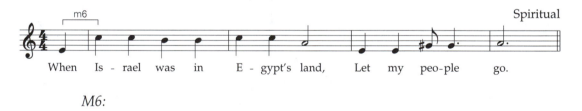

When Is - rael was in E - gypt's land, Let my peo - ple go.

M6:

HUSH, LITTLE BABY

Traditional

Hush, lit - tle ba - by, don't say a word. Ma-ma's gon-na buy you a mock-ing bird.

m7:

FORD JINGLE

Have you dri - ven a Ford, late - ly?

M7:

BALI HAI
from *South Pacific*

Oscar Hammerstein II
(United States, 1895–1960)

Richard Rodgers
(United States, 1902–1979)

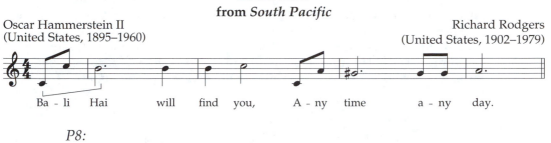

Ba - li   Hai   will   find   you,   A - ny   time   a - ny   day.

P8:

TAKE ME OUT TO THE BALLGAME

Jack Norworth

Albert von Tizel

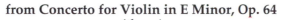

Take   me   out   to   the   ball   game,   Take   me   out with the   crowd. ____

PRACTICE

Identify each interval in these musical selections. The first measure is done for you.

SECOND MOVEMENT
from Concerto for Violin in E Minor, Op. 64
(theme)

Felix Mendelssohn
(Germany, 1809–1847)

FOURTH MOVEMENT
from *Peer Gynt* Suite No. 2

Edvard Grieg
(Norway, 1843–1907)

HAROLD IN ITALY

Hector Berlioz
(France, 1802–1869)

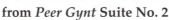

EMPEROR WALTZ
(theme)

Johann Strauss, Jr.
(Austria, 1825–1899)

* See page 202.

COMPOUND INTERVALS

Intervals larger than an octave are usually labeled *compound intervals*. The practice applies to intervals of a ninth, tenth, eleventh, twelfth, and so on. Compound interval names can be determined by first decreasing their size by an octave. The *simple interval* that results is the name added to *compound* when naming the larger interval. Here are several examples for you to study. Observe that the lower note in each case is raised one octave to determine the interval's size and quality.

Ninths:

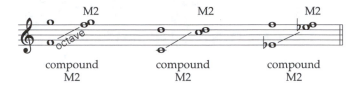

Tenths:

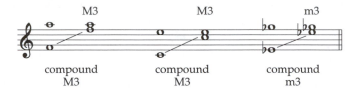

Elevenths:

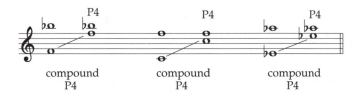

Twelfths:

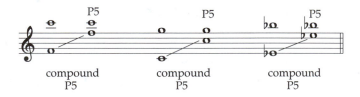

PRACTICE

Naming Compound Intervals

Reduce each compound interval by an octave to determine its name.

Compound _____   Compound _____

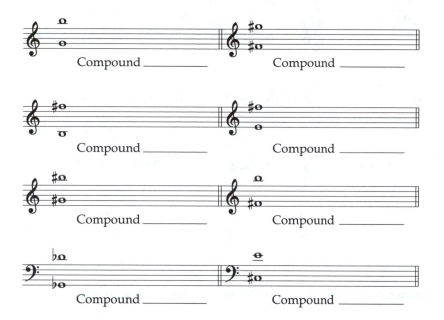

Compound _____   Compound _____

Compound _____   Compound _____

Compound _____   Compound _____

Compound _____   Compound _____

INTERVAL INVERSION

An interval can be inverted. Study these examples.

The sum of an interval and its inversion is nine. Major intervals inverted become minor intervals and vice versa. Perfect intervals inverted remain perfect. Study these examples.

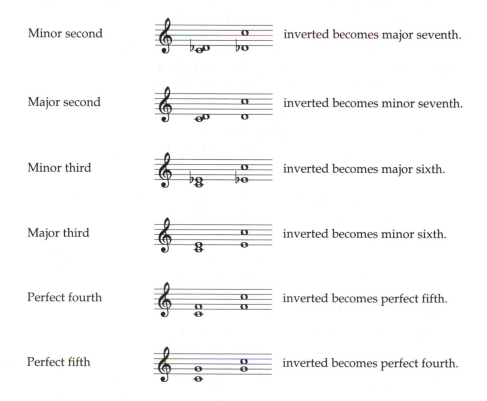

Minor second   inverted becomes major seventh.

Major second   inverted becomes minor seventh.

Minor third   inverted becomes major sixth.

Major third   inverted becomes minor sixth.

Perfect fourth   inverted becomes perfect fifth.

Perfect fifth   inverted becomes perfect fourth.

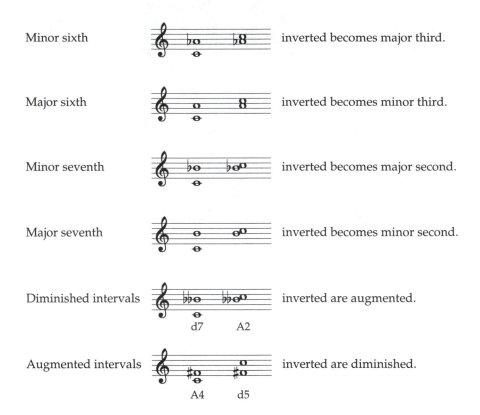

Minor sixth — inverted becomes major third.

Major sixth — inverted becomes minor third.

Minor seventh — inverted becomes major second.

Major seventh — inverted becomes minor second.

Diminished intervals — inverted are augmented.
d7   A2

Augmented intervals — inverted are diminished.
A4   d5

REVIEW OF TERMS

Define each term. Where appropriate, notate or use in a musical context to demonstrate your understanding.

1. interval
2. numerical identification
3. unison, prime
4. interval of a second
5. interval of a third
6. interval of a fourth
7. interval of a fifth
8. interval of a sixth
9. interval of a seventh
10. octave
11. melodic interval

12. harmonic interval
13. interval quality
14. perfect interval
15. major interval
16. nondiatonic interval
17. augmented interval
18. diminished interval
19. minor interval
20. compound interval
21. tritone
22. interval inversion

WORSHEET
Chapter 8 Review

Identifying and Playing Harmonic and Melodic Intervals

Identify each interval, naming both its size and its quality. You may use abbreviations (M2, m3, P4, A6, d5, and so on). Then play each one on a keyboard.

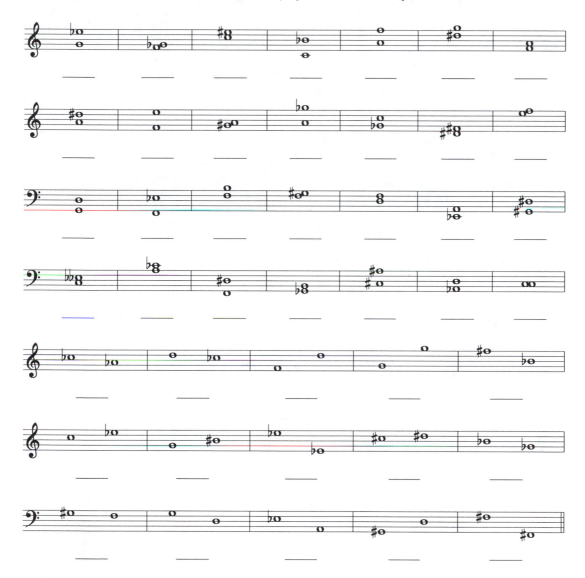

Writing Test: Intervals

Write the upper note for each interval.

P5   d4   M3   m6   P4   A2

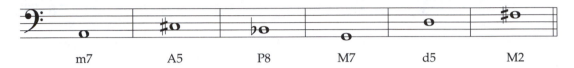

m7   A5   P8   M7   d5   M2

Write the lower note for each interval.

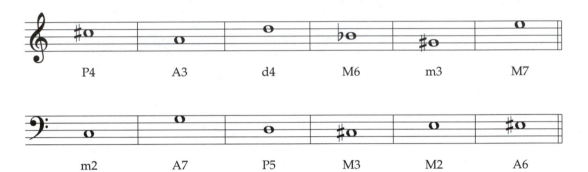

P4   A3   d4   M6   m3   M7

m2   A7   P5   M3   M2   A6

Write an enharmonic equivalent for each interval. Identify the size and quality of each one.

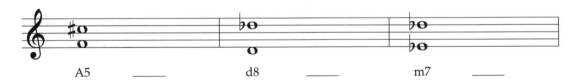

A5   _____   d8   _____   m7   _____

CHAPTER PROJECTS

1. Locate folk songs, art songs, opera arias, or solo instrumental pieces that begin with these intervals: prime, minor second, major second, perfect fourth, perfect fifth, minor sixth, major sixth, minor seventh, and octave.

2. Draw brackets over the melodic intervals in the excerpt from Mendelssohn's Symphony No. 4 on p. 129. Identify each interval.

3. See p. 97, Reading and Singing Melodies. Draw brackets over the melodic intervals in exercises 3–6. Identify each interval. Then play the first pitch of each exercise on a keyboard and sing on "loo" the remainder of the pitches.

4. Notate pitches using the following intervallic sequence. Then add rhythm and rewrite it as a melody. The first note is middle C.

↑P5 ↑P4 ↓P4 ↑M2 ↓M2 ↓M2 ↓m2 ↑m3 →P1 ↓P4 ↑M6 ↑m2 ↓P4 ↓m3 ↓M3

C __ __ __ __ __ __ __ __ __ __ __ __ __ __ __

5. Choose intervals from this group to sing or play at a keyboard for a partner to identify. Then reverse roles. Move exercise to different keys.

P1 m2 M2 m3 M3 P4 P5 m6 M6 m7 M7 P8

Triads, Chords, and Beginning Harmony

In this chapter on the basics of beginning harmony, you will learn how to construct triads and chords, and you will study their function in the accompaniment of melody. Although the scope of this text permits the exploration of only the most rudimentary harmonic concepts, the working knowledge you will have acquired by the end of the chapter will allow you to read and notate chordal accompaniments for much of the folk and popular music you will encounter and to discern the harmonic movement that underlies art music.

To understand the role of harmony in music, think of melody as the horizontal movement of sounds from left to right on the musical score and of harmony as a vertical element that enhances melody. These are analogous to the warp and woof of threads in fabric.

DINAH

MUSICAL APPLICATION

Singing a Song with Harmonic Accompaniment

Sing "Dinah," following the top line introduced by the treble clef. Then listen as your instructor plays at a keyboard the left-hand chords introduced by the bass clef. Now hum the song's melody as your instructor plays this harmonic accompaniment. You are performing *homophonic* music, defined as melody with accompaniment.

HARMONY, CHORDS, AND TRIADS

Harmony, a basic element in twentieth-century Western music, is a relative newcomer in the history of world musics. Rhythm and melody together flourished without harmony in single-line chants for many hundreds of years. Those chants are an example of *monophonic,* or single-line, music.

GREGORIAN CHANT

Music was transformed gradually, beginning about the ninth century, as monastery choirs added second lines to their chants. That earliest *homophonic* music was the first use of harmony, which is the simultaneous combination of two or more sounds. The chants were doubled at the interval of the perfect fourth or the perfect fifth.

Sit   glo – – ri – a   Do – mi – ni   in   se – cu – la

By the middle of the fifteenth century, the third was added to the fifth as a matter of common use, thereby creating the *chord,* which is defined as three or more pitches performed simultaneously. A chord comprising three sounds, built in thirds, forms a *triad.* Triadic harmony provides the basic accompaniment to melody in Western music.

SELECTED TRIADS

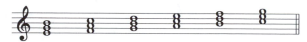

Root Position Triads: Root, Third, Fifth

Each note of a major or minor scale serves as the *root,* or lowest-sounding note, of a triad in *root position.* The middle note of the triad is called the *third,* and the top note is the *fifth.* The triads of the C major scale are shown below.

Triads on the C Major Scale in Root Position

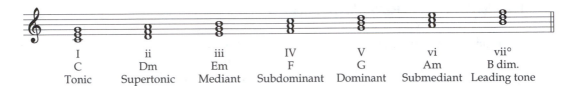

I	ii	iii	IV	V	vi	vii°
C	Dm	Em	F	G	Am	B dim.
Tonic	Supertonic	Mediant	Subdominant	Dominant	Submediant	Leading tone

Major Triads in a Major Key: Primary Triads   Study the triads and labels shown above. Observe that the *tonic* (I), the *subdominant* (IV), and the *dominant* (V) triads are major triads, indicated with uppercase letters and roman numerals. In a major triad, there is a major third between the root and the third, and a minor third between the third and the fifth. For example, in the major triad built on C, C–E is a major third, and E–G is a minor third. The major triads are called *primary triads* because of their important roles in harmonic structure.

Minor and Diminished Triads in a Major Key: Secondary Triads   In a major key, the *supertonic,* the *mediant,* and the *submediant* triads are minor, indicated with the lowercase letter *m* and lowercase roman numerals. In a minor triad, there is a minor third between the root and the third, and a major third between the third and the fifth. For example, in the minor triad built on D, D–F is a minor third, and F–A is a major third.

The vii triad, or leading tone triad, in a major key is *diminished,* with a minor third between the root and the third, and another minor third between the third and the fifth. For example, in the diminished triad built on B, B–D is a minor third, and D–F is also a minor third. The diminished triad is indicated by the abbreviation *dim.* or the symbol °. The minor and diminished triads are called *secondary triads.*

PRACTICE

Locating Triads on a Keyboard

Play the triads built on the C major scale. Sing them from the lowest to the highest notes—for example, (1) C, E, G, (2) D, F, A, (3) E, G, B. Practice until you can hear clearly the differences between major, minor, and diminished triadic qualities.

PRACTICE

Notating Triads

Notate triads above each note of the major scales shown here. Use appropriate uppercase and lowercase letters to identify them; then assign each triad a roman numeral and use ° or *dim.* if the triad is diminished.

Triads on the F major scale:

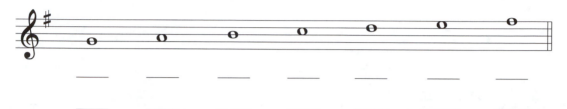

Triads on the G major scale:

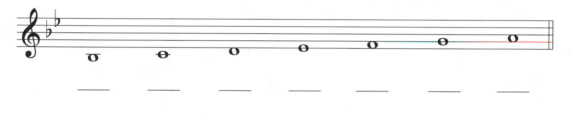

Triads on the B-flat major scale:

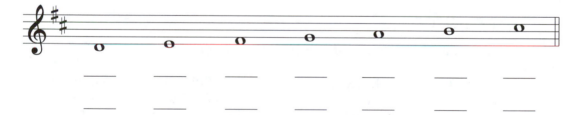

Triads on the D major scale:

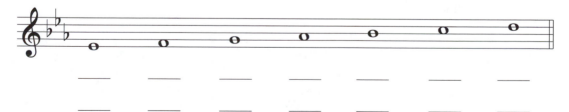

Triads on the E-flat major scale:

PRACTICE

Notating and Identifying Triads in Major Keys

Notate the triads that correspond to the roman numerals shown below each staff. Then add the correct uppercase and lowercase letters for major and minor triads or the abbreviation *dim.* for the vii triad.

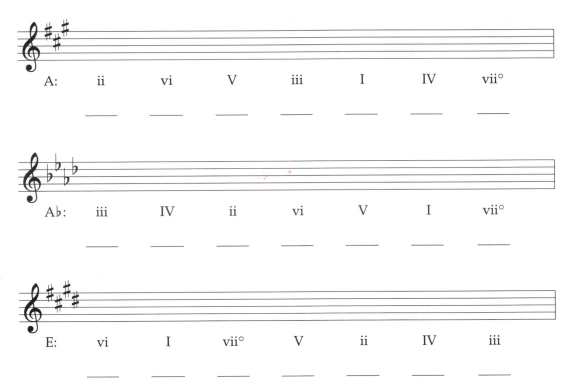

A: ii   vi   V   iii   I   IV   vii°

_____ _____ _____ _____ _____ _____ _____

A♭: iii   IV   ii   vi   V   I   vii°

_____ _____ _____ _____ _____ _____ _____

E: vi   I   vii°   V   ii   IV   iii

_____ _____ _____ _____ _____ _____ _____

PRACTICE

Notating the Thirds of Major and Minor Triads

Notate the third of each triad. The root and the fifth are shown. Remember that if the root and the fifth are in spaces, the third will also be in a space; if the root and the fifth are on lines, the third will also be on a line. In major triads, the root and the third form a major third, or comprise four half steps. In minor triads, the root and the third form a minor third, or three half steps. The lowercase *m* indicates a minor triad.

Examples:

3 half steps
^ ^ ^
G G♯ A B♭

Gm

4 half steps
^ ^ ^ ^
G G♯ A A♯ B

G

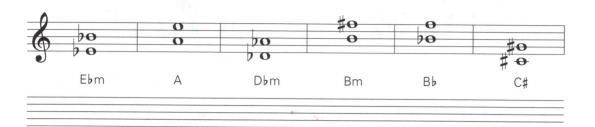

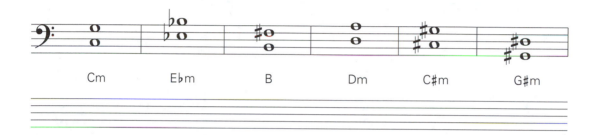

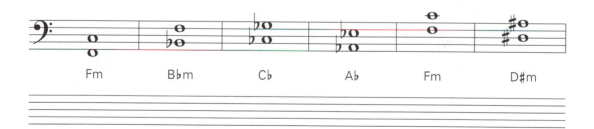

PRACTICE

Identifying Major and Minor Triads on a Keyboard

Study each triad indicated by the X's on the keyboard. Write one triad name that is associated with each example. Use *m* after the letter name of the triad's root if the triad is minor.

Cm

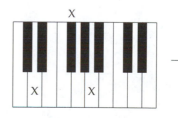

_____

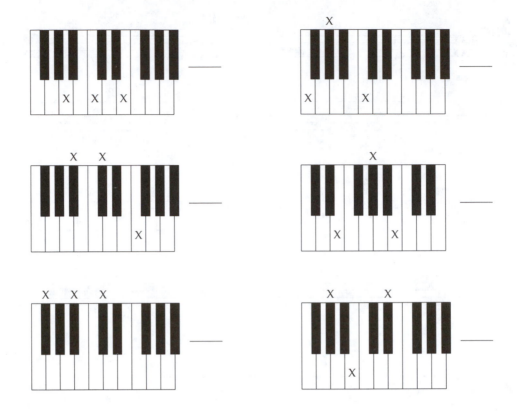

Chord Quality

Augmented Triads   The characteristic sound of a triad (for example, "major" or "minor,") is its quality. An augmented triad has its own sound. It is indicated by the symbol + or the abbreviation *Aug.* The augmented triad is made up of two major thirds. The distance from the root to the uppermost note of the triad is an augmented fifth, or eight half steps.

PRACTICE

Notating Augmented Triads

Write augmented triads based on the root notes shown here. Label them.

Diminished Triads   Remember from your practice with vii chords that diminished triads are made up of two minor thirds. The distance between the root and the uppermost note of the diminished triad is a diminished fifth, or six half steps.

PRACTICE

Notating Diminished Triads

Write diminished triads based on the root notes shown here. Label them.

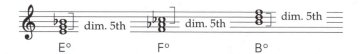

_____   _____   _____   _____   _____

PRACTICE

Identification of Chord Qualities

Identify the quality of each triad. After writing the letter name of the root, use *m*, +, or ° to indicate minor, augmented, or diminished triad structures. An uppercase letter by itself indicates a major triad.

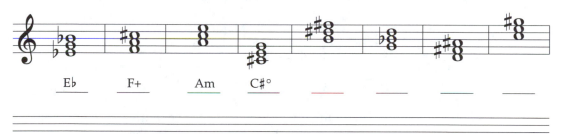

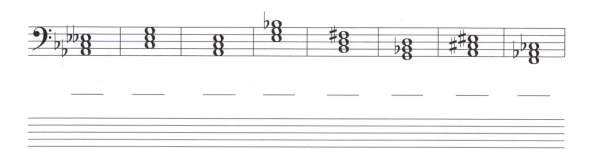

_____ _____ _____ _____ _____ _____ _____ _____

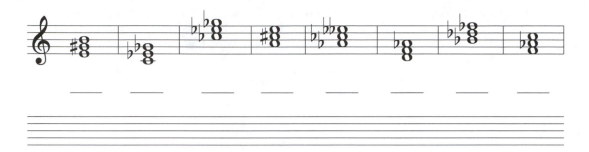

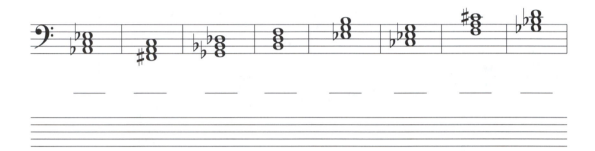

Seventh Chords and Dominant Seventh Chords

A third added above a triad creates a *seventh chord,* so named because the added note is at the interval of a seventh above the root. The most commonly used seventh chord is the *dominant seventh,* which adds a third to the V chord. The roman numeral or letter identification of the chord is shown with an added 7, as in V7 or G7.

When a triad appears on the lines of the staff, the seventh above the root will also be on a line; when a triad is in the spaces of the staff, the seventh above the root will be in a space.

PRACTICE

Notating Dominant Seventh Chords

Notate dominant seventh chords in the designated major keys. Remember to find the fifth degree of the key's scale first. That note will be the root of the dominant seventh chord. Then write its roman numeral and letter identifications in the space below the notation.

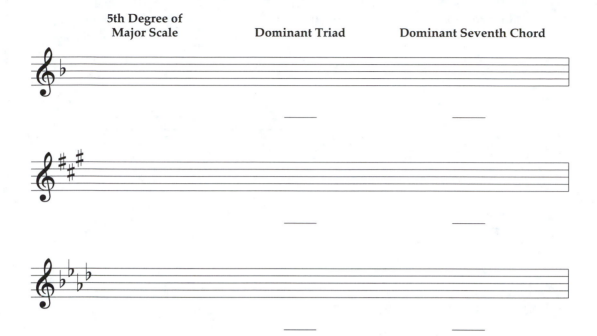

Triad Inversions

In the previous exercises, you notated triads in *root position*—that is, with the root tone in the lowest position. Triads may also appear in inverted position, with either the third or the fifth in the lowest position. When the third of a chord is notated in the lowest position, the triad is in *first inversion;* when the fifth appears in the lowest position, the triad is in *second inversion*. Study these examples of inverted triads. Then complete the Practice section that follows.

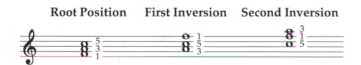

PRACTICE

Writing Triad Inversions

These triads are shown in root position. Write them in their first and second inversions as indicated.

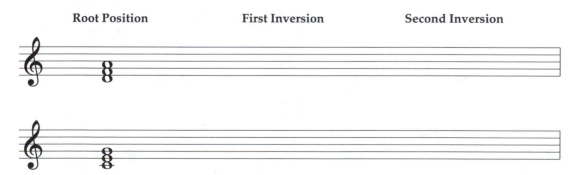

Root Position   First Inversion   Second Inversion

Inverted Dominant Seventh Chords

Seventh chords, like triads, can be inverted. Three inversions are possible. Study these examples.

Root position   First inversion   Second inversion   Third inversion   Root position   First inversion   Second inversion   Third inversion

Dominant seventh chords appear frequently with three notes: the root, the third, and the seventh. The fifth is omitted. Study these examples.

F: D:

MUSICAL APPLICATION

Accompanying in a Major Key with Primary Chords

"Swing Low, Sweet Chariot" can be accompanied with the three primary chords in G major. In the following score, the chords are written for left-hand accompaniment. The I chord, G-B-D, labeled G above the melody, is in root position. The IV chord, C-E-G, labeled C above the melody, is in second inversion. The V7 chord, D-F♯-A-C, labeled D7, is played without the fifth and is in first inversion. Observe that the inversions allow the performer to move easily from chord to chord. Locate the chords on a keyboard and play the accompaniment while a classmate or the group sings.

SWING LOW, SWEET CHARIOT

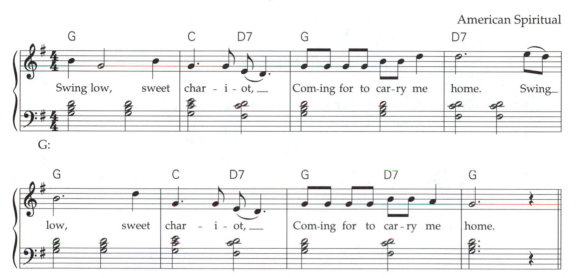

American Spiritual

Figured Bass

Baroque composers (1600–1750) used a system called *figured bass* to indicate chord inversions for keyboard players. In the practice of the time, only the bass note was shown and the keyboardist filled in the harmony by following the arabic numerals beneath the bass line. This approach is used today primarily in academic settings for harmonic analysis.

Triad inversions are identified with these figures: 5, 6, 6. The numbers repre-
                                                   3 3 4
sent the distances from the lowest-sounding note of a triad to its other notes.

A triad in root position, *though usually not labeled,* would be 5. The top note is
                                                                  3
a fifth above the root, and the middle note is a third above the root.

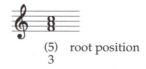

(5) root position
 3

First-inversion triads are indicated by the numerals 6. The top note is a sixth
$$3$$
above the root, and the middle note is a third above the root. *This is commonly abbreviated to include just the numeral 6.*

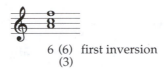

6 (6) first inversion
  (3)

Second-inversion triads are indicated by the numerals 6. The uppermost note
$$4$$
is a sixth above the root, and the middle note of the triad is a fourth above the root.

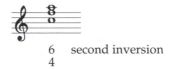

6 second inversion
4

Here are primary triads and their inversions in D-flat major and A major.
They are shown with figured bass.

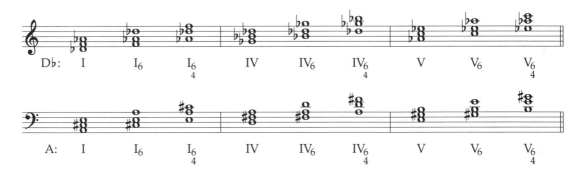

Db: I I_6 I_6^4 IV IV_6 IV_6^4 V V_6 V_6^4

A: I I_6 I_6^4 IV IV_6 IV_6^4 V V_6 V_6^4

PRACTICE

Notating with Figured Bass

Complete each major or minor triad by filling in its middle note. Lowercase
letters denote minor keys.

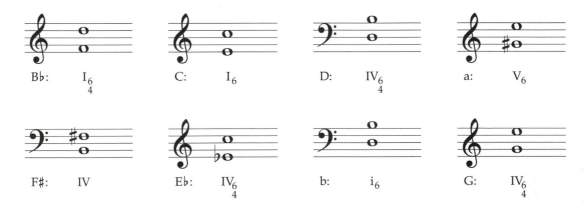

Bb: I_6^4 C: I_6 D: IV_6^4 a: V_6

F#:   IV   Eb: IV_6^4 b: i_6 G: IV_6^4

PRACTICE

Write major triads, observing the figured bass. Each note shown is the lowest-sounding note of a triad. Remember that the absence of numerals indicates root position.

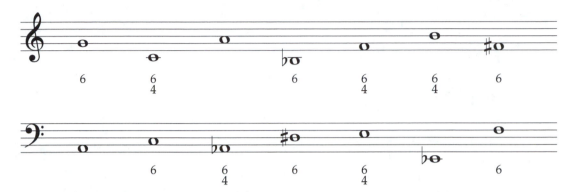

Figured Bass with Dominant Seventh Chords   In seventh chords, the figured-bass numerals are again determined by the distance of the uppermost notes from the lowest note. The V7 chord is an abbreviated 7.

(5)
(3)

F: V7

The first inversion, 6, is abbreviated to 6.

   5   5
(3)
(1)

F: V₆
     5

The second inversion, (6), is abbreviated to 4.

   4   3
   3
(1)

F: V₄
     3

The third inversion, (6), is abbreviated to 4 or 2.

F: V₄
         2

PRACTICE

Label these seventh chords with figured bass. The first one in each group is in root position and is labeled V7.

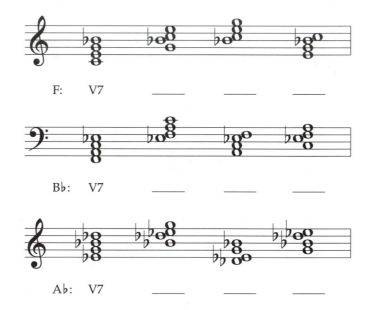

F: V7   _____   _____   _____

B♭:   V7   _____   _____   _____

A♭:   V7   _____   _____   _____

SUMMARY OF SYMBOLS FOR TRIAD AND SEVENTH CHORD INVERSIONS

	Triad Symbol	Seventh Chord Symbol
Root Position	none	7
First Inversion	6	6 5
Second Inversion	6 4	4 3
Third Inversion	none	4 2 or 2

MUSICAL APPLICATION

Locate on a keyboard the chords that appear after the bass clef in "Worried Man." The root position is shown beside the IV 6 and V 6 chords. Play the chords
with your left hand as your classmates sing or hum the song.

WORRIED MAN

Triads in Open Position

You have been studying and writing triads in *close position*, each with two thirds, one shown above another. Triads may also be written in *open position*, with greater distances between the notes. Study these examples; then complete the Practice section to write chords in both positions.

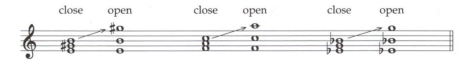

PRACTICE

Notating Triads in Open and Close Position

For each triad shown in close position, write its equivalent in open position; for each triad shown in open position, write its equivalent in close position. Designate each one as *M, m, A,* or *d.* Then play all the triads on a keyboard.

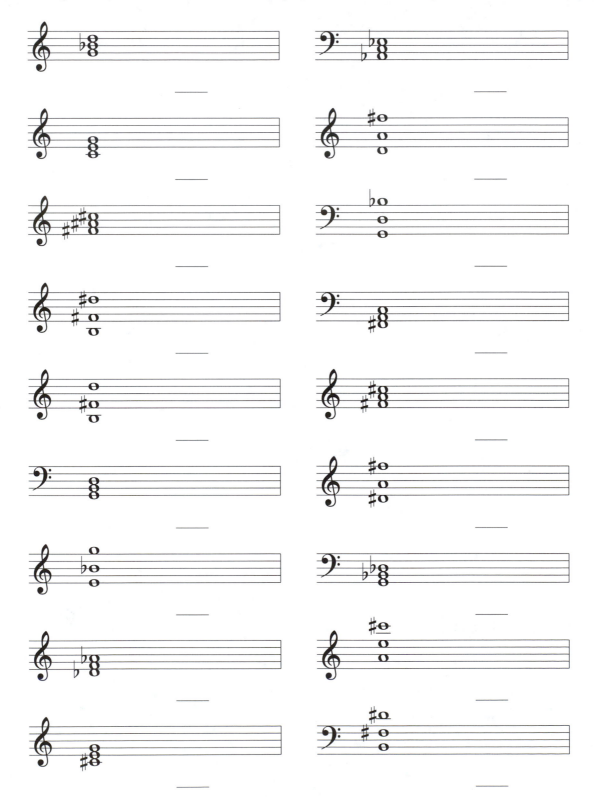

Doubling

Most music presents more than three notes sounding at a given time. The notes of a triad are doubled to make this possible. Notice in the examples here that the root, the third, or the fifth may be doubled.

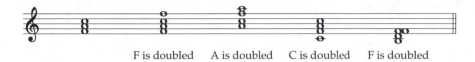

F is doubled   A is doubled   C is doubled   F is doubled

In choral scores, four parts are written on a grand staff and represent soprano, alto, tenor, and bass voices. The soprano and tenor parts are presented with the stems up; the alto and bass parts are shown with the stems down.

The ranges for the four voices are as follows:

PRACTICE

Identifying Doubled Notes

Study the following scores and circle the notes that are doubled.

Nonchord Tones

Nonchord tones, also called *nonharmonic tones*, are those pitches that are not part of the prevailing harmony. They contribute to the flow and beauty of a melody but move toward chord tones. Because of their momentary presence, usually on weak beats, chord changes are not needed to accommodate them. The most common nonchord tones are *passing tones* and *neighboring tones*.

Passing tones connect two pitches that are a second or a third apart, either ascending or descending. The abbreviation for passing tone is *p.t.*

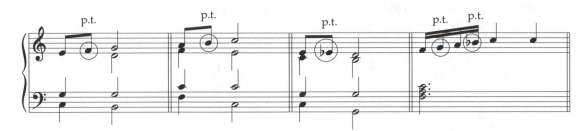

Neighboring tones are found between two identical pitches. If a neighboring tone is above the pitches, it is an upper neighbor; if it is below the pitches, it is a lower neighbor. The abbreviations for neighboring tones are *u.n.* and *l.n.*

PRACTICE

Labeling Nonchord Tones

The nonchord tones in the musical examples on pages 227 and 228 are marked with asterisks. Study them; then label them *p.t.*, *u.n.*, or *l.n.* Mark the nonchord tones in the following example.

PRACTICE

Reading Primary Chords in Musical Scores

Listen as your instructor or a classmate performs each excerpt. The I chord is the harmonic basis upon which each excerpt is built. Note that in actual music, triad tones may appear twice or even three times simultaneously. Find examples of open-position triads here. In the second excerpt, circle the notes that are not part of the I triad, *the nonchord tones.*

FIRST MOVEMENT
from Symphony No. 3

The root of E♭
appears 3 times.

Ludwig van Beethoven
(Germany, 1770–1827)

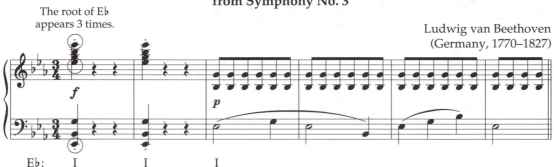

E♭:   I   I   I

FIRST MOVEMENT (R-54)
from Piano Sonata in F Major, K. 547

The root of F
appears 3 times

Wolfgang Amadeus Mozart
(Austria, 1756–1791)

Allegro

F: I   I   I

* = nonchord tones

Chord Progression

In these excerpts, either two (I, V) or three (I, IV, V) chords form the basic harmonic structure. The I chord is the most restful, and the V or the V7 is the most
active and tension-producing. The IV chord plays an intermediary role in the
tension-release heard in the movement from I to V and back to I. The succession
of chords in a composition is called a *chord progression*. The progression in the
Chopin mazurka is I–IV–I–V7–I–IV–I–V7–I. What are the progressions in the other
two excerpts?

MAZURKA, OP. 17, NO. 1 (R-55)

Frédéric Chopin
(Poland, 1810–1849)

Vivo e risoluto

B♭:   I   IV   I   V7   I

(continued)

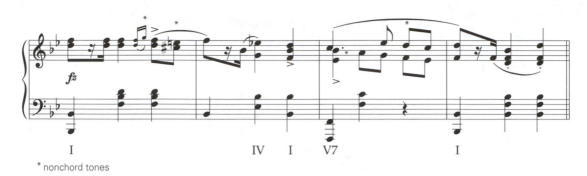

I   IV   I   V7   I

* nonchord tones

THIRD MOVEMENT (R-56)
from Sonatina in F Major

Franz Joseph Haydn
(Austria, 1732–1809)

* nonchord tones

NOCTURNE, OP. 37, NO. 1 (R-57)

Frédéric Chopin
(Poland, 1810–1849)

Eb: I IV   I   IV I V I   V I IV I   V vi V7 I

Triads Constructed on the Harmonic Minor Scale

The harmonic form of the minor scale is frequently used in the application of harmonic principles to minor keys. Study the following triads, built on the E harmonic minor scale.*

*All F's and D's in the triads on E harmonic minor are sharp.

	i	ii°	III+	iv	V	VI	vii°
	Em	F#dim.	G aug.	Am	B	C	D#dim.
	Tonic	Supertonic	Mediant	Subdominant	Dominant	Submediant	Leading tone

PRACTICE

Writing Triads on Harmonic Minor Scales

Notate the triads indicated after each key name. Write the sharps and flats of the triads as accidentals rather than as key signatures. Then write the upper-case and lowercase letters under the triads, indicating *dim.* where diminished and *aug.* where augmented.

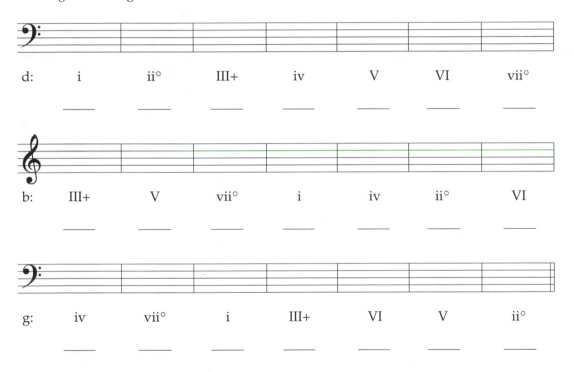

Dominant Seventh Chords in Minor Keys

Dominant seventh chords in minor keys are notated identically to those in major keys because the notes of the harmonic minor scale are used to create the chords in minor. This results in a major third in the V triad, to which the seventh is added. Study this example.

Scale of C Harmonic Minor

Dominant Seventh Chord in C Minor

PRACTICE

Notating Dominant Seventh Chords

Notate dominant seventh chords in the designated minor keys. Use accidentals rather than key signatures. Remember to find the fifth degree of the key's scale first. That note will be the root of your dominant seventh chord. The bottom interval of the dominant seventh chord in a minor key should be *major*.

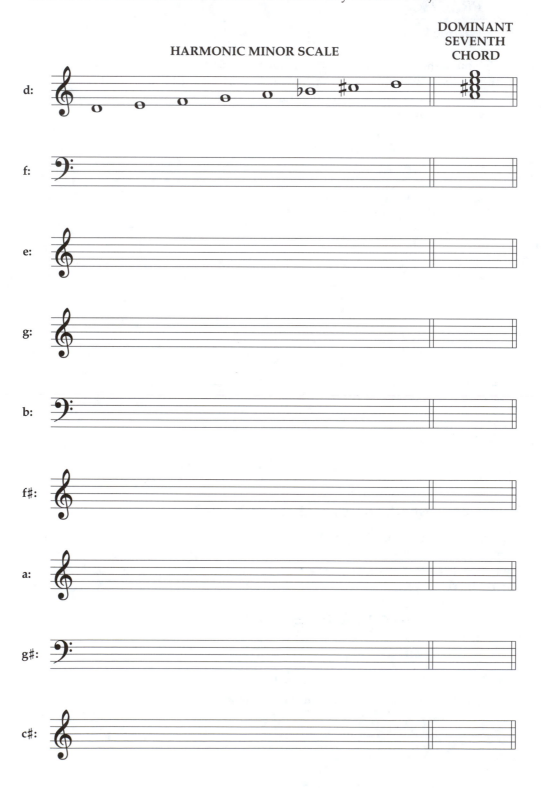

bb: 𝄢

PRACTICE

Write the name of a key associated with each dominant seventh chord shown here. Remember that the chord's root is the dominant, or fifth note, of the key's scale.

MUSICAL APPLICATION

Accompanying in a Minor Key with Primary Chords

"Let My People Go," presented here in E minor, can be accompanied by the three primary chords in that key. The i chord, E-G-B, is in root position. The iv chord, A-C-E, appears in second inversion, and the V7 chord, B-D♯-F♯-A, is in first inversion. Remember that the primary chords contain all the notes of a key, making it possible to coordinate the chords with the notes of a melody in that key. Find the note in each chord that corresponds to the notes in the melody. Then play the three chords on a keyboard while your classmates sing or hum the song.

LET MY PEOPLE GO

African-American Spiritual

(continued)

PRACTICE

Reading Primary Chords in Minor Keys

In this excerpt, listen for the movement from V to i. If the performer stops on the V chord, this section of the composition sounds incomplete.

ALBUM FOR THE YOUNG, OP. 68, NO. 12

Robert Schumann
(Germany, 1810–1856)

* nonchord tones

WALTZ, OP. 18, NO. 5 (R-58)

Franz Schubert
(Austria, 1797–1828)

* nonchord tones

Cadences in Music

You have seen how the tonic and the dominant seventh chords work to provide harmonic pillars in folk music and art music. Dominant harmony creates tension that is resolved when the tonic chord is heard.

Motive, Phrase, Half Cadence, Authentic Cadence, Period   In a typical musical structure of eight bars, a *motive* is presented in two or more notes. The composer manipulates the motive to fashion a melody. The motive may be repeated, or repeated in a different position, or inverted, and so on. The first four measures are a *phrase* that concludes with a *half cadence,* I–V7, which conveys a feeling of incompleteness. The second group of four measures "answers" the first phrase and ends on the tonic chord with an *authentic cadence.* The entire eight-measure group is called a *period.* In a double period, the first ends on dominant harmony, and the second on tonic harmony, with a total of sixteen measures.

PRACTICE

Study the following examples. The first is a period of two phrases; the second is a double period with two phrases in each period.

ODE TO JOY
from Symphony No. 9, fourth movement

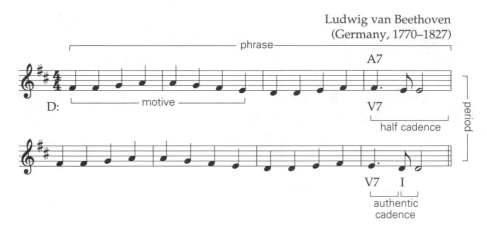

Ludwig van Beethoven
(Germany, 1770–1827)

FIRST MOVEMENT (R-59)
from Symphony No. 104 (London)
(excerpt)

Franz Joseph Haydn
(Austria, 1732–1809)

MUSICAL APPLICATION

Period Analysis

Study the following example. Mark with brackets the motive, phrases, half cadence, and authentic cadence.

THE WILD RIDER
from Album for the Young, Op. 68, No. 8
(excerpt)

Robert Schumann
(Germany, 1810–1856)

Plagal Cadence   Another type of cadence, the *plagal cadence,* includes IV–I harmonic movement and is often referred to as the "Amen" cadence. It is used frequently after an authentic cadence to conclude a hymn or a sacred work.

PRACTICE

Notating Cadences

Study the chords in the following cadences. Then write them in the keys indicated beneath the staves.

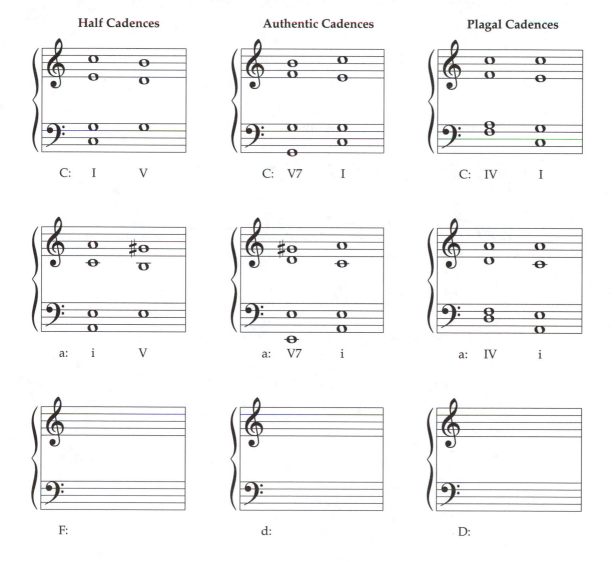

Half Cadences	Authentic Cadences	Plagal Cadences
C: I V	C: V7 I	C: IV I
a: i V	a: V7 i	a: IV i
F:	d:	D:

HARMONIZING MELODIES

Although the composer/arranger chooses chords from a vast harmonic palette, many tunes, particularly those in the folk, commercial, pop, and hymn repertoires, can be accompanied with simple chord progressions using the primary chords. The student who has learned the basic progressions well can then modify them into a variety of styles.

Study the following examples and play them on a keyboard. Practice with the right-hand and then the left-hand models. Finally, play them together.

PRIMARY CHORD PROGRESSIONS

Primary Chord Progression in C Major

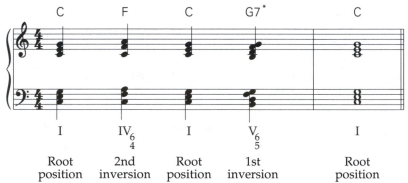

Primary Chord Progression in A Minor

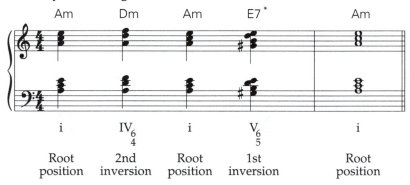

* The fifth may be omitted.

PRACTICE

Notating Primary Chord Progressions

Complete the notation for the following chord progressions. Play them on a keyboard until you can perform them smoothly at a moderate tempo.

Primary Chord Progression in G Major:

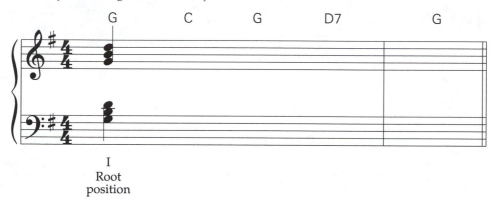

Primary Chord Progression in E Minor:

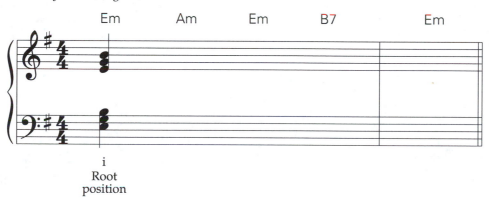

Primary Chord Progression in F Major:

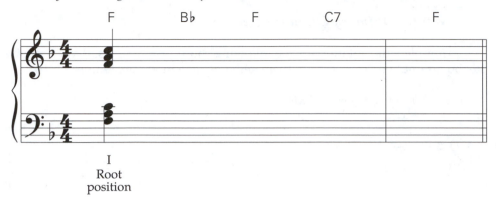

Primary Chord Progression in D Minor:

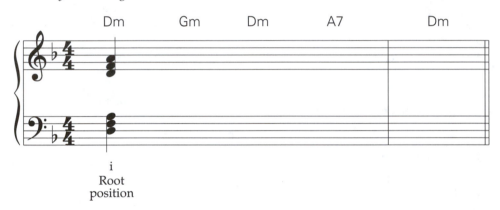

Primary Chord Progression in D Major:

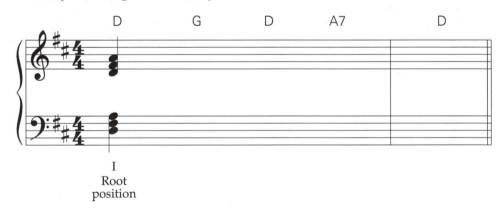

Primary Chord Progression in B Minor:

Primary Chord Progression in B♭ Major:

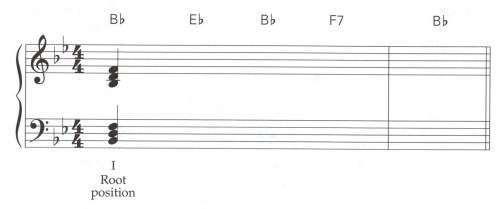

I
Root
position

Primary Chord Progression in G Minor:

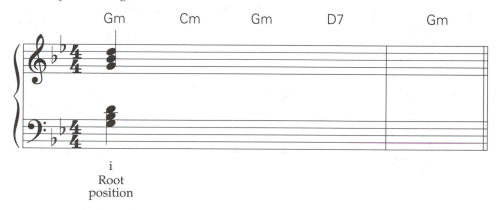

i
Root
position

Styles of Chordal Accompaniments

Block-Chord Accompaniments Block-chord accompaniments present the chords on the strong beats, or on every beat, to provide both rhythmic and harmonic movement. Practice the left-hand chordal accompaniment for this song. Then sing the song and play the accompaniment. Finally, play the chords with both hands and accompany a singer or a group.

Block-chord style:

KUM BA YAH

Black American

Root-Triad Accompaniments   Sometimes chord roots appear on the first beat of a measure and the entire chord is used on the secondary accent of the measure, as in "Shoo, Fly, Shoo." Sing the song; then play the accompaniment while you sing or to accompany others.

SHOO, FLY, SHOO

Root-triad style:

Broken-Chord Accompaniments   Chords may be broken, with the root or the bottom note of a first inversion appearing alone on the first beat and the upper notes of the chord sounding on the remaining beats. Practice this duet style with a partner playing the melody.

Broken-chord style:

OLD TEXAS

They've got no use _____ for the long-horn cow. _____

V7   I

Arpeggiated Accompaniments   The notes of chords may also sound in arpeggiated style, one at a time, to provide a smooth, continuous flow. See the measures following "I'm on My Way." Play them several times. Then follow the chord names over the measures to accompany the song.

I'M ON MY WAY

Black American Song

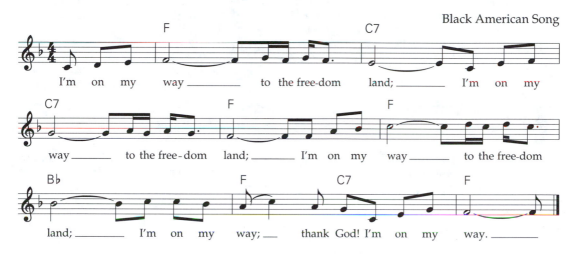

I'm on my way _____ to the free-dom land; _____ I'm on my

way _____ to the free-dom land; _____ I'm on my way _____ to the free-dom

land; _____ I'm on my way; __ thank God! I'm on my way. _____

Arpeggiated style:

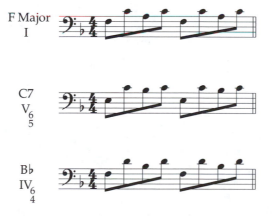

Accompanying a Blues Song   You can accompany a blues song with a typical twelve-bar *blues progression*. You can begin with "St. Louis Blues," page 173. The song is in G major, and the twelve bars have chords in this sequence:

G:	G	G	G	G7	C	C	G	G	D7	C	G	G
Bar	1	2	3	4	5	6	7	8	9	10	11	12

MUSICAL APPLICATION

Notating and Performing Accompaniments

Notate block-chord or root-triad accompaniments for the following songs. Follow these steps:

1. Write out the primary chords in the key of the song. Write the letter names of each note in each chord.
2. Examine the notes of each measure. Which notes are prevalent and on the strong beats? Which chord has the same notes?
3. Circle the notes that are passing tones or neighboring tones in the melody. Remember that these notes do not indicate the need for a new chord.
4. Notate keyboard chords for the left hand on the first beat of each measure. Sing the song with the chords you have now.
5. Fill in the other chords as needed. Remember that the I and V7 chords appear more often than the IV chord. The songs end on the tonic (I) chord.

OH, SUSANNA

Stephen Foster
(United States, 1826–1864)

1. I ___ come from Al - a - ba - ma with my ban-jo on my knee, Oh I'm
2. It ___ rained all night the day I left, The wea-ther it was dry, The ___

goin' to Lou' - si - an - a my ___ true love for to see.
sun so hot I froze to death, Su - san - na don't you cry.

Refrain

Oh, Su - san - na, Oh, don't you cry for me, For I

come from A - la - ba - ma with my ban - jo on my knee.

SIMPLE GIFTS

Shaker Hymn

Songs in this text that you can harmonize include the following:

Key	Song Title
Dm	A La Nanita Nana, p. 5
G	All God's Children Got Shoes, p. 171
F	Crawdad, p. 58
Dm/F	Erie Canal, p. 126
G	Good King Wenceslas, p. 13
F	Red River Valley, p. 88
Cm	Sometimes I Feel Like a Motherless Child, p. 150
Dm	Wayfaring Stranger, p. 73
C	When the Saints Go Marching In, p. 85
G	Amazing Grace, p. 73
G	On the Bridge at Avignon, p. 16
D	Tom Dooley, p. 148
F	Kum Ba Yah, p. 63
D	Michael, Row the Boat Ashore, p. 62
G	She'll Be Comin' Round the Mountain, p. 53
C	Old Smoky, p. 56
G	Down in the Valley, p. 142

REVIEW OF TERMS

Define each term. Where appropriate, notate or use in a musical context to demonstrate your understanding.

1. monophonic music
2. Gregorian chant
3. homophonic music
4. chord
5. triad
6. root of a triad
7. third of a triad
8. fifth of a triad
9. tonic triad
10. subdominant triad
11. dominant triad
12. root position
13. major triad
14. minor triad
15. diminished triad
16. augmented triad
17. seventh chord
18. dominant seventh
19. chord quality
20. triad inversion
21. first inversion
22. second inversion
23. figured bass
24. 6, $^6_4$
25. $V6_5$, $V4_3$, $V4_2$
26. open-position chord
27. primary chords
28. chord progression
29. harmonizing a melody (harmonization)
30. neighboring tone
31. passing tone
32. authentic cadence
33. half cadence
34. plagal cadence
35. block-chord accompaniment
36. broken-chord accompaniment
37. arpeggiated accompaniment

WORKSHEET
Chapter 9 Review

1. What is the difference between monophonic and homophonic music?

_____

_____

2. Notate the primary triads in F major.

3. Notate the first inversion and the second inversion of each triad.

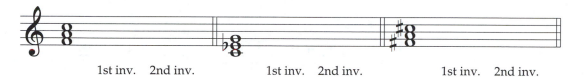

 1st inv.   2nd inv.   1st inv.   2nd inv.   1st inv.   2nd inv.

4. Write the dominant seventh chord of each key.

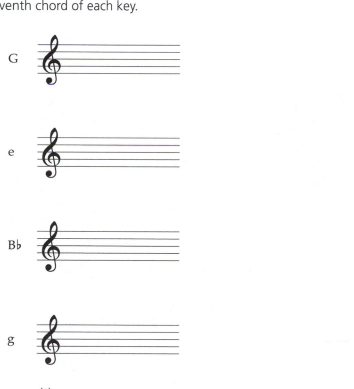

G

e

B♭

g

5. Notate each triad in open position.

6. Notate the triads named below the staff.

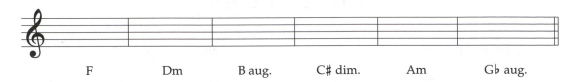

F   Dm   B aug.   C♯ dim.   Am   G♭ aug.

7. Notate the chord progression in F major indicated below the staff.

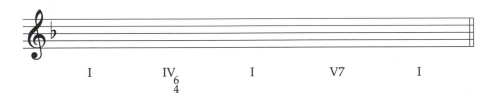

I   IV₆₄   I   V7   I

8. Notate the chord progression in A minor indicated below the staff.

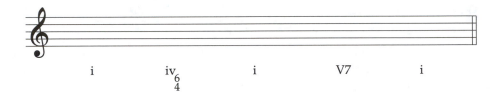

i   iv₆₄   i   V7   i

9. What procedure would you use to provide a harmonic accompaniment for this melody?

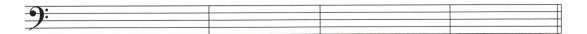

10. Write a block-chord keyboard accompaniment for the melody shown in question 9.

11. Notate these triads following the figured bass.

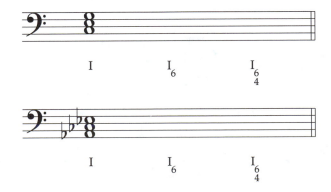

12. Number these triads in the order they are performed.

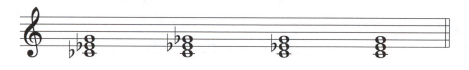

___ ___ ___ ___

13. Number these triads in the order they are performed.

___ ___ ___ ___

14. Complete each cadence indicated below.

Half cadence

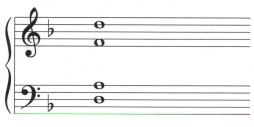

d:

Plagal cadence

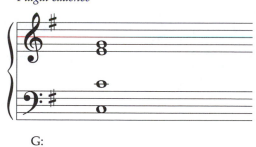

G:

Authentic cadence

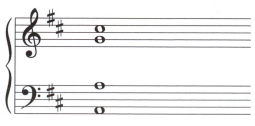

D:

15. Use roman numerals and numbers to identify the chords and chord inversions in this progression.

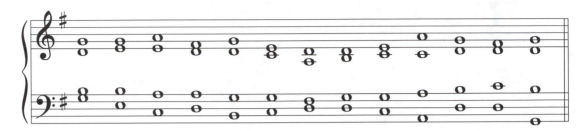

CHAPTER PROJECTS

1. Compose melodies that can be accompanied by these chords.

a.

b.

2. Find examples of half, authentic, and plagal cadences in hymns and in eighteenth-century keyboard sonatas. Bring to class for analysis.

Relative Note Values

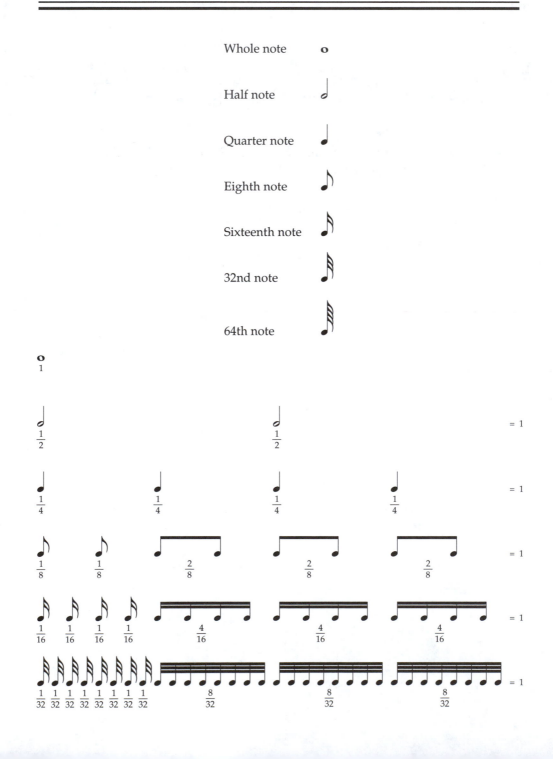

Whole note	o
Half note	♩
Quarter note	♩
Eighth note	♪
Sixteenth note	♬
32nd note	
64th note	

Conducting Patterns

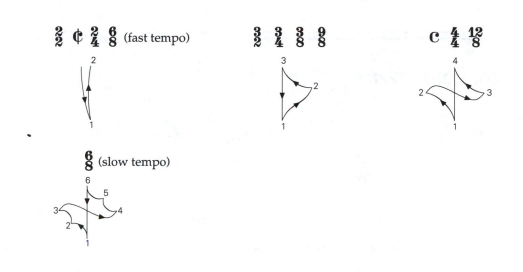

Musical Symbols and Terms

NOTATIONAL TERMS

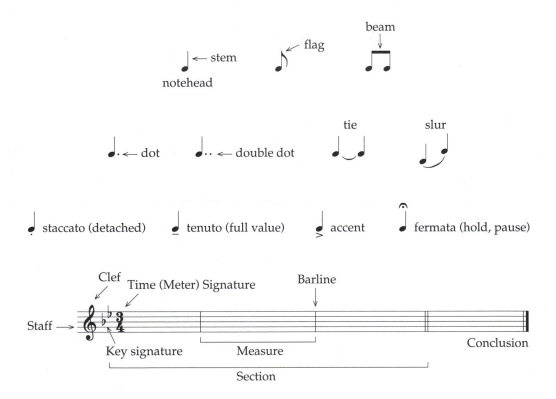

DIRECTIONAL SYMBOLS AND TERMS

Repeat sign: Go back to beginning and play again.

Repeat signs: Repeat material within the dots.

First and second endings: Play the first ending. Go back to the beginning
and play entire piece, this time omitting first ending and concluding with
second ending.

D.C. al Fine (Da capo al Fine): Repeat from the beginning, perform to the word
Fine (fee-nay, "end").

D.C. al Coda (Da capo al coda): Return to beginning and perform to the coda
sign ⊕. Go to coda and perform to end.

D.S. (Dal segno): Go back to the sign 𝄋 and perform to the end.

Ottava alta (8va): Perform an octave higher than written.

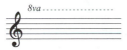

Ottava bassa (8va): Perform an octave lower than written.

SYMBOLS AND TERMS OF DYNAMICS

ppp (molto pianissimo)—extremely soft

pp (pianissimo)—very soft

p (piano)—soft

mp (mezzo piano)—moderately soft

f (forte)—loud

ff (fortissimo)—very loud

fff (molto fortissimo)—extremely loud

    ＜ *Crescendo (cresc.)*—gradually louder

    ＞ *Decrescendo (decresc.)*—gradually softer

    ＞ *Diminuendo (dim, dimin.)*—gradually softer

TEMPO TERMS

Largo—very slow
Lento—very slow
Adagio—relaxed pace
Andante—moderately
Moderato—moderately
Allegro—fast
Presto—very fast
Vivace—lively
Accelerando (accel.)—gradually faster
A tempo—return to original tempo
Rallentando (rall.)—gradually slower
Ritardando (rit.)—gradually slower
Ritenuto (riten.)—immediately slower
Rubato—deliberate unsteadiness of tempo

EXPRESSION TERMS

Animato—animated
Cantabile—in a singing style
Dolce—sweetly
Giocoso—joyfully
Grazioso—gracefully
Legato—connected
Maestoso—majestically
Sforzando—strong accent
Sostenuto—sustained

Additional directive terms are

Meno—less
Molto—much
Più, Peu—more
Poco—little
Poco a poco—little by little
Tutti—all

Keyboard Fingerings for Commonly Used Major and Minor Scales

PLAYING MAJOR AND MINOR SCALES

To play the C, G, D, and A ascending major scales and the A, D, G, C, and E ascending minor scales in the right hand, pass your thumb under your third finger. To play them in a descending pattern, pass your third finger over your thumb. The procedure is just the opposite for the left hand. To play the ascending scales, pass your third finger over your thumb. To play the descending scales, pass your thumb under your third finger. The F, B♭, and E♭ major scales and the B and F♯ minor scales require different fingerings.

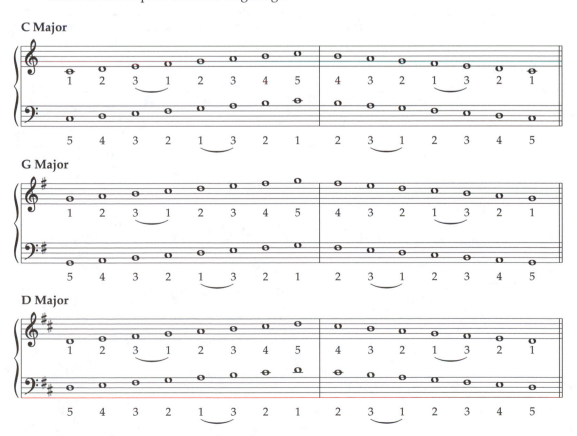

A Major

A Minor

D Minor, all forms

G Minor, all forms

C Minor, all forms

E Minor, all forms

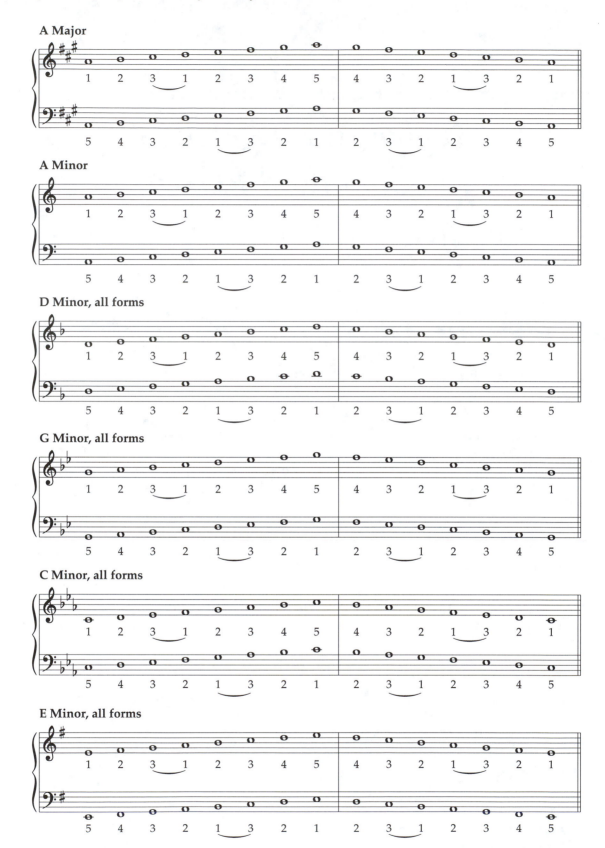

Different fingerings are required to play the B and F♯ minor and the F, B♭, and E♭ major scales:

B Minor, all forms

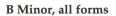
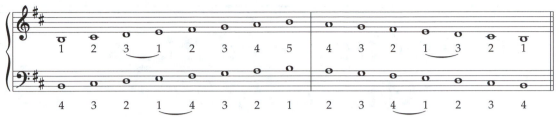

F-sharp Minor, all forms

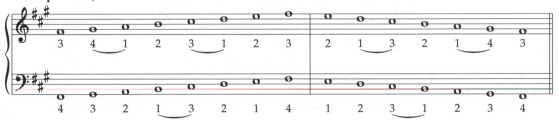

F Major

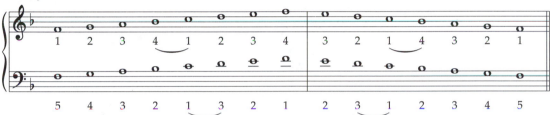

B-flat Major

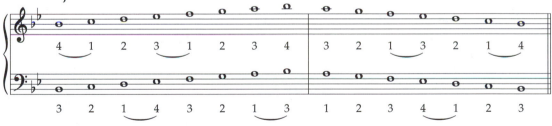

E-flat Major

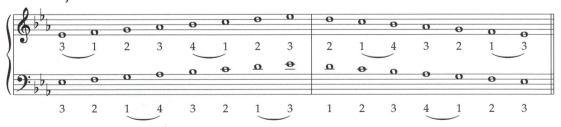

Circle of Fifths: Major and Minor Key Signatures

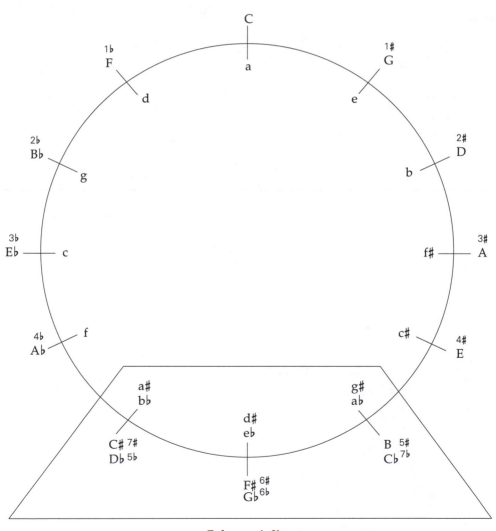

Enharmonic Keys

Computer Software
for Music Fundamentals

The software listed here is compatible with this textbook and reinforces the fundamentals, exercises, and projects presented in the nine chapters.

MiBac Music Software
P.O. Box 468
Northfield, MN 55057
Fax: 507–616–2377
800–645–3945
Internet: Info@mibac.com
Web:http://www.mibac.com

Music Lessons

IBM: Windows 3.1 or later. VGA or SVGA video display. MIDI optional. *Macintosh* Plus or later. System 6.0 or System 7. MIDI Optional

This program contains eleven drills, each with multiple skill levels. The student can select work in treble, bass, or alto clefs. The drills are: Note Names, Circle of Fifths, Key Signatures, Major/Minor Scales, Modes, Jazz Scales, Scale Degrees, Intervals, Note/Rest Durations, Ear-Training Intervals, Ear-Training Scales. Help screens explain each musical term necessary to master the drills. Progress reports provide detailed records of student scores and can be saved and printed.

Musicware
P.O. Box 2882
Redmond, WA 98073
Fax: 206–881–9664
800–997–4266

Guido Intervals

IBM

Sequenced, interactive, MIDI-optional drill-and-practice program. User control of parameters, including speed, timbre, melodic or harmonic intervals, ascending/descending/mixed presentation, fixed upper or lower notes, keyboard practice on screen. Instructor record-keeping available.

Music Lab

IBM-compatible 286-386 or newer computer with sound card, microphone, and VGA or later monitors. A DOS program. Works on Novell, Lantastic, and other networks. *Macintosh:* any with 32-bit logic capability and a microphone input jack (e.g., Quadra, Centris, SE30, PowerMac, and most Performa models).

An interactive tutoring system that teaches students to sing, read, and write music in twenty achievement levels through a spiral curriculum. Eight interrelated modules help students internalize pitch and rhythm skills. Three focus on pitch training, with passive reinforcement of rhythm skills: *Sing* teaches vocal pitch accuracy by "listening" to a student's singing voice and giving instant feedback; *Notes* drills on staff notation and solfeggio; *Names* concentrates on pitch recognition. Three of the modules teach rhythmic skills with passive reinforcement of pitch training: *Echo* teaches accuracy in rhythmic perception and response; *Play* drills rhythm reading; *Notate* teaches rhythm writing through rhythmic dictation. The *Read* and *Write* modules combine the component skills. Comprehensive record-keeping and teacher controls monitor student progress. Quizzes provide objective measurements of student progress.

Opcode Interactive
3950 Fabian Way, Suite 100
Palo Alto, CA 94303
415–494–1112

Claire

Macintosh: System 7 or higher, 2 MB RAM minimum. A 68020 LC computer or better. FPU, Macintosh microphone, or MacRecorder recommended.

Ear training and intonation are taught through a structured curriculum that is adjusted to each student's starting level, age, progress, and tessitura. The voice is used as a means of building an "internal ear." Student goals are production of in-tune pitches and the development of a sense of pitch recognition that includes practice with intervals, chords, and modes. The solfège exercises may be either Fixed *Do* or Movable *Do*.

Signature Music Software
3512 Waverley St.
Palo Alto, CA 94306
415–424–0390 or 800–865–8842
Signature 5 @ AOL.COM

The Music Maid

Macintosh: System 7 or higher.

A user-friendly notational program for the instructor or the student. Creates custom or predesigned worksheets. Useful for creation of papers with musical examples. Text is interspersed readily with scores. Includes exercises on rhythm, pitch, solfège syllables, harmony, intervals, and creative assignments.

Chronology of Major Composers and Events in Western Civilization

MIDDLE AGES (450–1450)

Composers	Historical and Cultural Events
	Sack of Rome by Vandals (455)
	Reign of Pope Gregory I (590–604)
Hildegard (1098–1179)	First Crusade (1096–1099)
Perotin (late twelfth century)	Beginning of Notre Dame Cathedral in Paris (1163)
	King John signs Magna Carta (1215)
Guillaume de Machaut (c. 1300–1377)	
	Hundred Years' War (1337–1453)
	Black death (1348–1350)

RENAISSANCE (1450–1600)

Composers	Historical and Cultural Events
Guillaume Dufay (c. 1400–1474)	Fall of Constantinople (1453)
Josquin Desprez (c. 1440–1521)	Columbus discovers America (1492)
	Martin Luther's ninety-five theses (1517)
Andrea Gabrieli (c. 1520–1586)	
Giovanni Pierluigi da Palestrina (c. 1525–1594)	Council of Trent (1545–1563)
Roland de Lassus (1532–1594)	
William Byrd (1543–1623)	
Giovanni Gabrieli (c. 1555–1612)	
Thomas Morley (1557–1603)	Elizabeth I, queen of England (1558–1603)
	Spanish Armada defeated (1588)
Thomas Weelkes (1575–1623)	

BAROQUE (1600–1750)

Composers	Historical and Cultural Events
	Jamestown founded (1607)
Claudio Monteverdi (1567–1643)	
Heinrich Schütz (1585–1672)	
Jean-Baptiste Lully (1632–1687)	Louis XIV reigns in France (1643–1715)
Arcangelo Corelli (1653–1713)	
Henry Purcell (c. 1659–1695)	Newton, *Principia Mathematica* (1687)
Elisabeth-Claude Jacquet de la Guerre (1666–1729)	
François Couperin (1668–1733)	
Antonio Vivaldi (1678–1741)	Louis XV reigns in France (1715–1774)
Johann Sebastian Bach (1685–1750)	
George Frideric Handel (1685–1759)	

CLASSICAL (1750–1820)

Composers	Historical and Cultural Events
	Maria Theresa reigns in Austria (1740–1780)
	Frederick the Great reigns in Prussia (1740–1786)
	Publication of the French *Encyclopedia* begins (1751)
Christoph Gluck (1714–1787)	
Carl Philipp Emanuel Bach (1714–1788)	Winckelmann's *History of the Art of Antiquity* (1764)
Joseph Haydn (1732–1809)	
	Louis XVI reigns in France (1774–1792)
Wolfgang Amadeus Mozart (1756–1791)	American Declaration of Independence (1776)
Ludwig van Beethoven (1770–1827)	French Revolution begins (1789)
	Eli Whitney invents cotton gin (1792)
	Napoleon becomes first consul of France (1799)
	Battle of Waterloo (1815)

ROMANTIC (1820–1900)

Composers	Historical and Cultural Events
Carl Maria von Weber (1786–1826)	
Gioacchino Rossini (1792–1868)	
Franz Schubert (1797–1828)	Revolutions in France, Belgium, Poland (1830)
Hector Berlioz (1803–1869)	
Fanny Mendelssohn (1805–1847)	First Reform Bill in Britain (1832)
Felix Mendelssohn (1809–1847)	
Frédéric Chopin (1810–1849)	Revolutions of 1848; Marx and Engels, *The Communist Manifesto* (1848)
Robert Schumann (1810–1856)	
	Darwin's *Origin of Species* (1859)
Franz Liszt (1811–1886)	American Civil War (1861–1865)
Richard Wagner (1813–1883)	Franco-Prussian War (1870)
Giuseppe Verdi (1813–1901)	
Clara Schumann (1819–1896)	
César Franck (1822–1890)	
Anton Bruckner (1824–1896)	

Composers *(cont.)*

Historical and Cultural Events *(cont.)*

Bedřich Smetana (1824–1884)
Johannes Brahms (1833–1897)
Georges Bizet (1838–1875)
Modest Mussorgsky (1839–1881)
Peter Ilyich Tchaikovsky (1840–1893)
Antonin Dvořák (1841–1904)
John Philip Sousa (1854–1932)
Cécile Chaminade (1857–1944)
Giacomo Puccini (1858–1924)
Gustav Mahler (1860–1911)
Richard Strauss (1864–1949)
Amy Beach (Mrs. H. H. A. Beach, 1867–1944)

First group exhibition of impressionists in Paris (1874)

Bell invents telephone (1876)

Spanish-American War (1898)

TWENTIETH CENTURY

Composers

Historical and Cultural Events

Airplane invented (1903)

Freud, *The Psychopathology of Everyday Life* (1904)

Claude Debussy (1862–1918)
Scott Joplin (1868–1917)
Arnold Schoenberg (1874–1951)
Charles Ives (1874–1954)
Maurice Ravel (1875–1937)
Béla Bartók (1881–1945)
Igor Stravinsky (1882–1971)
Anton Webern (1883–1945)
Edgard Varèse (1883–1965)
Alban Berg (1885–1935)

Einstein, special theory of relativity (1905)

World War I (1914–1918)
Russian Revolution begins (1917)
Women win voting rights in U.S.A. (1921)
Beginning of Great Depression (1929)
Franklin D. Roosevelt inaugurated (1933)
Hitler Chancellor of Germany (1933)

Sergei Prokofiev (1891–1953)
Bessie Smith (1894–1937)
Paul Hindemith (1895–1963)
George Gershwin (1898–1937)
E. K. ("Duke") Ellington (1899–1974)
Carlos Chavez (1899–1978)
Aaron Copland (1900–1990)
Ruth Crawford-Seeger (1901–1953)
Dmitri Shostakovich (1906–1975)
Elliott Carter (b. 1908)
Olivier Messiaen (1908–1992)
John Cage (1912–1992)
Benjamin Britten (1913–1976)
Billie Holiday (1915–1959)
Milton Babbit (b. 1916)
Leonard Bernstein (1918–1990)
Charlie Parker (1920–1955)
Pierre Boulez (b. 1925)
Karlheinz Stockhausen (b. 1928)

World War II (1939–1945)

Atomic bomb destroys Hiroshima (1945)
Korean war begins (1950)

John F. Kennedy assassinated (1963)
American involvement in Vietnam increases (1965)

Composers *(cont.)*

Historical and Cultural Events *(cont.)*

George Crumb (b. 1929)

Krzysztof Penderecki (b. 1933)   American astronauts land on moon (1969)

Mario Davidovsky (b. 1934)

Steve Reich (b. 1936)

Charles Wuorinen (b. 1938)   Resignation of President Nixon (1974)

Philip Glass (b. 1937)

Ellen Taaffe Zwilich (b. 1939)   End of American involvement in Vietnam (1975)

Libby Larsen (b. 1950)

United States and China establish diplomatic relations (1979)

Revolution in Iran (1979)

Wars in Lebanon and the Falkland Islands (1982)

Nuclear accident at Chernobyl, Soviet Union (1986)

Berlin Wall opened (1989)

Bosnian War (1992–

NASA launches Mars Global Surveyor (1996)

Glossary

accent   Emphasis on a note; indicated by a wedge-shaped mark (< or >) or the note's placement in a measure.

accidental   A symbol placed before a note on the staff that changes the pitch for one measure: flat (lowers pitch one half step); sharp (raises pitch one half step); natural (cancels previous sharps and flats).

Aeolian mode   One of the church modes of the Medieval and Renaissance periods; can be played on the piano by sounding the white keys from A to A. Survives today as the natural minor scale.

alla breve (¢)   A tempo mark indicating $\frac{2}{2}$ meter instead of $\frac{4}{4}$; quick duple time with the half note rather than the quarter note as the beat. See also *cut time.*

alto clef   See *C clef.*

anacrusis   An incomplete measure occurring before the first complete measure of a musical work.

asymmetric meter   Meter in which the beat groupings are irregular, as in $\frac{5}{4}$ or $\frac{7}{4}$.

augmented interval   An interval one half step larger than the major or perfect interval of the same name.

augmented triad   A three-note chord comprising two major thirds.

authentic cadence   The progression of the dominant V chord to the tonic I chord to complete a section or a composition.

bar line   A vertical line on the staff used to separate measures.

Baroque period   The period in music history from about 1600 to about 1750.

bass clef, F clef (𝄢)   A symbol that identifies the fourth line of the staff (from the bottom) as the position of F. Used for notes below middle C.

beam   A horizontal line used to connect stems of notes.

beat   The basic pulse of a musical composition.

blue notes   The name applied in jazz music to the third and seventh degrees of the scale, which are used both natural and flatted and frequently with a deliberate sliding sound in between.

blues progression   Twelve measures comprising a succession of chords used in blues music:

```
1  2  3  4   5    6  7  8  9    10   11  12
I  I  I  I  IV  IV  I  I  V  V/IV   I    I
```

blues scale   A major scale in which the third and seventh degrees are lowered one half step.

cadence   A series of chords that brings a sense of completion to a musical phrase.

C clef (𝄡)   A symbol indicating the position of C on the staff. A C clef on the third line is called the *alto clef;* on the fourth line, it is the *tenor clef.*

chord   Three or more tones sounded simultaneously.

chromatic scale   A scale of twelve half steps.

circle of fifths   A visual aid for learning key signatures and key names for major and minor keys. Adjacent key signatures are arranged in a circular sequence with tonic keys one perfect fifth apart.

clef   A sign placed at the beginning of the staff to designate the the position of some particular pitch on the staff and, by extension, the other pitches of the staff's lines and spaces. From the Latin *clavin,* meaning "key."

common time   An alternative term for $\frac{4}{4}$ meter; notated with the symbol **C** .

compound interval   An interval that comprises an octave and another interval. An octave with an added second is a ninth; an octave with an added third is a tenth; and so on.

compound meter   A meter in which the subdivision of the beat is in three, as in $\frac{6}{8}$, $\frac{9}{12}$, or $\frac{12}{4}$.

contour   The shape of a melody.

crescendo   Gradually becoming louder; indicated by the symbol ⟨ .

cut time   A term indicating the $\frac{2}{2}$ time signature; notated with the symbol ¢ . See also *alla breve.*

D.C. al Fine (Da Capo al Fine)   An instruction to the performer to return to the beginning of the musical score and sing or play to the word *Fine* ("end").

decrescendo   Gradually becoming softer; indicated by the symbol ⟩ .

diatonic scale   A scale of five whole steps and two half steps comprising all the letter names of the musical alphabet.

diminished interval   An interval one half step smaller than a perfect or a minor interval.

diminished triad   A triad made up of two minor thirds, with a diminished fifth between the root and the fifth of the triad.

dissonance   An interval that creates a feeling of instability and requires a movement toward resolution. Seconds and sevenths are dissonant.

dominant   The fifth pitch class in a scale; the fifth degree of a scale.

dominant seventh chord   A four-note chord constructed on the fifth, or dominant, note of a scale. Consists of the root, third, and fifth of the major triad with an additional note a minor seventh above the root.

Dorian mode   One of the church modes of the Medieval and Renaissance periods; can be played on the piano by sounding the white keys from D to D. Like a natural minor scale with a raised sixth degree.

dot   A symbol placed beside the notehead to increase a note's duration by one half.

double flat (♭♭)   A symbol indicating that a pitch is to be lowered one whole step.

double sharp (x)   A symbol indicating that a pitch is to be raised one whole step.

drone   The simultaneous sounding of the first and fifth degrees of the scale in a repeated rhythmic figure as an accompaniment for a chant or a song. Also called "bordun."

D.S. al Fine (Dal Segno al Fine)   An instruction to the performer to return to the sign 𝄋 and to perform from the sign to the word *Fine* ("end").

duple meter   A meter in which the beat units are grouped into two, such as $\frac{2}{2}$ or $\frac{2}{4}$.

duplet   Two equal notes performed in the time normally given to three in compound meter.

duration   The length of a tone.

enharmonic pitches   Pitches of the same frequency but with different letter names, such as B-flat and A-sharp.

F clef   See *bass clef.*

fermata (𝄐)   A sign placed above a note indicating a hold or a pause.

figured bass   A system of chord notation developed during the Baroque period in which the bass line is provided with arabic numbers (figures) indicating chords and their inversions.

fine   Italian term meaning "the end."

first inversion   The rearrangement of a chord's notes so that the third displaces the root. For example, C-E-G becomes E-G-C.

flat (♭)   A symbol indicating that a pitch is to be lowered one half step.

forte (f)   Loud, strong.

fortissimo (ff)   Very loud.

grand staff   Two staves joined by a vertical line and a bracket; displays treble and bass notes simultaneously. Sometimes called the "great staff."

half cadence   A cadence ending on the dominant (V) chord.

half step   The smallest interval written in notation; a semitone.

harmonic minor scale   A form of the minor scale in which the seventh degree has been raised one half step. The pattern of whole steps and half steps is: whole, half, whole, whole, half, whole + half, half.

harmony   The vertical arrangement of pitches into intervals, triads, and chords.

homophonic   Characterized by a single melodic line supported by chordal or more elaborate accompaniment.

improvisation   Musical performance that is spontaneous, without aid of memorization or notation.

interval   The distance between two tones. The name is determined by counting all pitch names within that distance.

inversion   The rearrangement of the notes of a chord so that the root does not appear as the lowest tone.

Ionian mode   One of the church modes of the Medieval and Renaissance periods; can be played on the piano by sounding the white keys from C to C. Survives today as the major scale.

key   The tonic of the scale on which the melody is constructed.

key signature   The sharps or flats at the beginning of the staff indicating the key or scale associated with the composition.

leading tone   The seventh pitch class of a major, harmonic minor, or melodic minor scale.

ledger line   A line that extends the staff to accommodate notes above the fifth line or notes below the first line.

legato   A connected, smooth manner of performance.

Lydian mode   One of the church modes of the Medieval and Renaissance periods; can be played on the piano by sounding the white keys from F to F. Like a major scale with a raised fourth degree.

major scale   A scale in which the pattern of whole steps and half steps is: whole, whole, half, whole, whole, whole, half. The scale used most frequently in Western music.

major triad   A three-note chord with a major third between the root and the third, and a minor third between the third and the fifth.

measure   An area of the staff enclosed by bar lines; includes beats in groupings indicated by the meter (time) signature. Sometimes referred to as a "bar."

measure repeat sign (𝄎)   A symbol that instructs the performer to repeat the preceding measure.

mediant   The third pitch class, or degree, of a scale.

melodic minor scale   A minor scale in which both the sixth and the seventh degrees are raised one half step in the ascending form: whole, half, whole, whole, whole, whole, half. The descending form is identical to the descending natural minor: whole, whole, half, whole, whole, half, whole.

melodic syllables   Syllables used in sight-reading melodies. The first, *do*, is assigned to the tonic of a scale. The order of syllables is *do, re, mi, fa, sol, la, ti, do* in major and *la, ti, do, re, mi, fa, sol, la* in minor.

melody   A planned series of pitches moving forward in time.

Medieval period   The period from about 500 to about 1420. Sometimes referred to as the Middle Ages. "Early" Western music is from this period and the Renaissance.

meter   The grouping of beats and the organization of strong and weak pulses within the grouping.

meter signature   See *time signature.*

metronome   A mechanical device used by performers to keep beats steady at a specific pace often designated by the composer of a work.

middle C   The C close to the middle of the piano keyboard and indicated on a ledger line between the two staves of the grand staff.

minor interval   A major interval reduced in size by one half step. Only seconds, thirds, sixths, and sevenths are minor.

minor scale   A scale characterized by its half step between the second and third degrees.

minor triad   A triad with a minor third between the root and the third, and a major third between the third and the fifth.

Mixolydian mode   One of the church modes of the Medieval and Renaissance periods; can be played on the piano by sounding the white keys from G to G. Like a major scale with a lowered seventh degree.

monophonic   Characterized by a single melodic line without other parts or accompaniment.

natural (♮)   A symbol that cancels a sharp or a flat that appears earlier in the score.

natural minor scale   A minor scale in which the pattern of steps is: whole, half, whole, whole, half, whole, whole. The Aeolian mode.

octave   An interval in which two pitches have the same letter name (for example, A–A), with one pitch at twice the frequency of the other.

octave sign (*8va*)   A symbol that instructs the performer to play the notes one octave higher (if positioned above the notes) or lower (if positioned below the notes) than written.

parallel keys   Major and minor scales that have the same tonic note but different key signatures.

passing tone   A tone positioned between chord tones in a melody.

pentatonic scale   A five-tone scale with this pattern: M2, M2, m3, M2.

perfect interval   An interval quality name given to unisons, fourths, fifths, and octaves.

period   A structured section of music including a "question," which ends on a half cadence, and an "answer," which ends on an authentic cadence.

phrase   A musical segment with an identifiable beginning and ending. May be compared to a clause in speech.

Phrygian mode   One of the church modes of the Medieval and Renaissance periods; can be played on the piano by sounding the white keys from E to E. Like a minor scale with a lowered second degree.

pianissimo (pp)   Very soft.

piano (p)   Soft.

piano   A keyboard instrument. The name comes from the Italian *gravicembalo con piano e forte,* meaning a keyed instrument with both soft and loud tones.

pitch   A specific position in the range of sounds from low to high; caused by vibrations of a string, a column of air, or vocal cords; determined by number of vibrations per second.

plagal cadence   The progression of the subdominant chord (IV) to the tonic (I) chord. Also known as the "Amen" cadence.

primary chords   Chords built on the first, fourth, and fifth scale degrees of the major, harmonic minor, and melodic minor scales.

quadruple meter   A meter in which the beat units are grouped into four, such as $\frac{4}{2}, \frac{4}{4}, \frac{4}{8}$.

relative major   A major key that has the same key signature as its related minor key; a scale that begins on the third step of a minor scale.

relative minor   A minor key that has the same key signature as its related major key; a scale that begins on the sixth step of a major scale.

Renaissance period   A period in Western history from about 1420 to about 1600.

repeat signs (‖: :‖)   Symbols used to indicate that the music between the signs should be repeated.

rest   Silence within the sounds of music; a symbol with a specific duration related to a note.

rhythm   Patterns of long and short sounds and silences with durations related to a regular pulse.

ritardando (rit.)   Gradually delaying the beats.

root position   The arrangement of a chord's notes so that the root is the lowest note.

rubato   A style of performance in which one note value may be extended at the expense of another for purposes of expression.

scale   The linear succession of the seven pitch classes of a key, both ascending and descending; identified by specific patterns of half steps and whole steps.

secondary chords   The chords built on the second (II), third (III), sixth (VI), and seventh (VII) degrees of a major, harmonic, or melodic minor scale.

second inversion   The rearrangement of a chord's notes so that the fifth displaces the root. For example, C-E-G becomes G-C-E.

sharp (♯)   A symbol indicating that a pitch is to be raised one half step.

simple meter   A meter in which the subdivision of the beat is in two, as in $\frac{2}{4}, \frac{2}{8}$, or $\frac{4}{4}$.

slur   A curved line connecting noteheads of different pitches; denotes the smooth connection of notes in performance.

staccato   A detached manner of performance indicated by dots above or below noteheads; opposite of legato.

staff   A series of five equidistant horizontal lines on which pitches and rhythms are notated. See also *grand staff.*

subdominant   The fourth scale degree of a major or minor scale or the chord with the fourth scale degree as its root.

submediant   The sixth scale degree of a major or minor scale or the chord with the sixth scale degree as its root.

subtonic   The seventh degree of a natural minor scale; it is one whole step below the tonic.

supertonic   The second scale degree of a major or minor scale or the chord with the second scale degree as its root.

syncopation   Displacement of the accent from a strong to a weak beat.

tempo The pace of the beats in music.

tenor clef See *C clef.*

tie A curved line connecting identical pitches indicating that the duration of the first should be extended to include the second.

time signature The two numbers that appear after the clef and the key signature on the staff; the upper number indicates the number of beats per measure, the bottom number the beat unit. May be called "meter signature."

tonic The first scale degree or the chord with the first scale degree as its root. The source of a key name. "Tonality" is the relationship of the other tones in a scale to the tonic.

tonic sol-fa A system of musical notation using melodic syllables to aid in sight singing. The tonic of the scale is always *do.* Also called "movable *do.*" Different from "solfeggio," in which C is always *do.*

transposition The process of moving the notes in a piece of music from one key to another.

treble clef, G clef (𝄞) A symbol that identifies the second line of the staff (from the bottom) as the position of G. Used for tones above middle C.

triad A three-note chord comprising two thirds.

triple meter A meter in which the beat units are grouped into three, such as $\frac{3}{2}, \frac{3}{4}, \frac{3}{8}$.

triplet Three equal notes performed in the time normally given to two in simple meter.

upbeat A weak beat that precedes the first strong beat, or downbeat, in a composition. See also *anacrusis.*

whole step An interval made up of two consecutive half steps.

whole-tone scale A scale of six whole steps.

Classified Index
of Music

Folk Music: World Sources

*Entire work is shown. All other selections are excerpts.

Composed Music

General Index